Tilde

A LITERARY JOURNAL

~

Vol. 3 Issue 1 ~ Summer 2020
An Imprint of *Thirty West Publishing House*

Tilde

~

EDITOR-IN-CHIEF

Josh Dale

MANAGING EDITOR	TE Tomaino
POETRY EDITOR	Carrie Soltner
FICTION EDITOR	Nick McMenamin
NON-FICTION EDITORS	Bob Kaplan
	Melissa DiGiovannantonio
COVER PHOTOGRAPHY	Rebecca Goodman

Tilde: A Literary Journal
Vol. 3 Issue 1~ Summer 2020

www.thirtywestph.com

ISBN-13 978-1-7345158-1-7
ISSN 2576-960x (Print)
ISSN 2576-9618 (Online)

CONTENTS

EDITOR'S NOTE

~

In light of recent historical events and the current climate in our city of Philadelphia, I decline writing an editor's note for this issue. Let the words speak for themselves; let each piece occupy a moment in your mind.

Thank you for reading and supporting marginalized voices around the world.

In solidarity,

~ TE Tomaino

June 2020

"I grieve the sorrow roar the sorrow sob
of many more left hand or right
black children and white
men the mountaintop the mob
I grieve the sorrow roar the sorrow sob
the fractured staring at the night

Sometimes America the shamescape
knock-rock territory losing shape
the Southern earth like blood
rolls valleys cold gigantic
weeping willow flood
that lunatic that lovely land
that graveyard growing
trees remark where men
another black man
died he died again
he died"

From "Who Look at Me" (1969), June Jordan (b.1936-2002)

B.H. PITT
XANADU IN AUGUST

Wednesday,
past midnight,
two lovesick owls
coo to each other
from separate trees
and predict rain
to lull the restless
into sleep.

They wonder, "who, who,
took away the moon?"

EGOR LEMAK
BUTTER*

there is so much butter in the summer.
it shines with soft glossy lumps,
it pastes itself with ice-cream sticks
on the scruffy faces of kids,
on their freckled, broiled backs.
the poplar fluff
sticks to the burned butter so easily.
the yard swells, smells, spills broth
like a huge field kitchen.
toy soldiers made of tin and butter
are baking sand biscuits
when the commander shouts,
"to arms! to arms!"
they grab some branches,
and hurry forward through the yellow boiling broth
and then disperse into the poplar fluff.
"get off my flowerbeds!" a neighbor shouts.
an old woman grumbles,
"I remember the time when
one could kill, get married, or give herself
for thirty grams of butter.
oh, yes, I remember that."

oh dear,
it's so scary and upsetting.
it grieves so much to think of them,
of all of them, alive and real

The field kitchen quiets down by night,
and the butter thickens
on the flowerbeds, on the windows,
on the sleepy back of kids,
on the old woman's mumbling dream.

*Translated by Sergey Gerasimov from Russian

RACHEL NOLAN
LAST SUPPER

The last time I saw you alive
you made pasta by hand.
Fingers accustomed to sin
tenderly folded flour and eggs
for our personal Eucharist:
the body and blood and garlic.
Your homemade creation myth
swapped apples with tomatoes
which stained your apron a medley
of North Stars. But back to your hands
kneading the dough. I remember them
like this, instead of ashes at the altar.
The last time I saw you alive,
we were our own Three Kings with gifts
indistinguishable from warmth
or sacrifice. Judas was not with us
but at his own table, waiting.
We were not concerned. We feasted.
It was holy. Between mouthfuls
we talked of times we didn't know
would never come.

There were two nuns. They were nuns who were alcoholics who wrote short stories. One was an unremarkable Protestant nun who let the light of God shine through her and tried her best to forget her own authorship—both of her short stories and her actual life. The other was the first Jewish nun. She had chosen faith in God to quell obsessive thoughts and become a better writer. Both liked techno quite a bit. At one time they had thought it was the search for a secular God. One loved men too much; the other hated. The problem was their ruminative personalities (which you will just have to trust me on; there is no time to demonstrate their ruminative personalities). It made them prime candidates for becoming devout.

They did things like drink themselves into oblivion, wear no clothes in the cold till their ears stung (just one nun did this), eat only acai bowls and only once every three days, and beat themselves viciously with riding crops. This was ostensible to bring them closer to God, but, really, both took pleasure in their own pain. One nun had serious philosophical contemplations regarding the epistemology of pain – experiencing pain as confirmation, observing pain as doubt – while the other nun really just tried hard to be a flute. For God to play on – you know how it goes with these types.

Occasionally they would down a bottle of brandy and make lists of their own qualities. They had many qualities. They would burn these lists.

I wasn't yet hip to Captain's habitual disappearing act. He was incommunicado and I was pissed. I cried. I got pissed off because I cried. I worried. And hoped. *Maybe Captain scared himself into getting help. Maybe he's with his friend...the guy who quit drinking and is going to AA meetings and lives in Ohio. That's why Captain hasn't called. He left Florida to go get help in Ohio. Oh, wait! The AA guy lives in the same town, down the same street as my ex-husband...*Rattled and tattered, unable to separate hope and fantasy, I began attending weekly Al-Anon meetings in the wake of idiotically asking my former husband if he could flush out any information from his neighbor, Captain's possible prehab host.

The Al-Anon group was small. Three, sometimes four women. I listened to their survivor war stories; they listened to my skirmish woes. The meeting room had an oversized Twelve Step list taped on the paneling. Every week I stared at the poster. The principles looked complicated, demanding, and unattainable. I could admit to Step One. Sure as rocks are hard and water is wet, my life had indeed become unmanageable. Step Two was horrifying. Come to believe a greater Power could restore my sanity? That would require confronting my biggest fear and admit I was insane. And no way could I do all the God stuff. "Keep coming back" was the veterans' levelheaded encouragement.

Day by day, little by little, I assimilated Step One; agreed I was up shit creek against alcohol. I blamed the recent trouble on booze-related incidents, brought on by the boozer. I was fresh to the program, an Al-Anon amateur who thought responsibility and culpability were the same things. I chipped away at dumping worry and fear and useless what-ifs. After all, if the queen had balls she would be king.

I plodded up one side of Al-Anon, down the other, and paid visits for tutorials at AA meetings open to guests. On an intellectual level, I wrapped my head around the programs' content but resisted when my heart knotted in an enigma. Better than choking on paradox, asphyxiating on speculative contradictions, I could've used some sort of beginner's translator. A decoder ring attached to the conference approved *How Al-Anon Works*. Dial-in the confusing parts and get easy to swallow solutions. Just give me the answers so I could move on with my life.

The notion of hope blew all other ambiguity, confusion, and frustration out of the water. Webster's dictionary defines hope as "a feeling of expectation and desire for a certain thing to happen". Al-Anon warns expectations are premeditated resentments.

Webster says hope "can be a person or thing that may help or save someone". "Keep coming back" to Al-Anon hoping to save an alcoholic is a dead-end into a brick wall. Hold off beating that horse before someone gets hurt.

The dictionary illustrates hope as grounds for believing something good may happen, unsupported by recovery failure statistics. The dismal rehab industry success rate, between five and ten percent, is not widely publicized, adding up to ninety percent who fall and don't get up. Nine out of every ten who shoulder their lapse as another character defect. Another reason to feel damned and deviant. *Hey, Loser! Obviously, you didn't want the help bad enough.*

Al-Anon is worse. Getting clean is a cakewalk compared to the exorcism for sober mental health, the Al-Anon coursework. Participants offer triumphant anecdotes as favorable rehabilitation proof in a structure missing observable improvement measurements like abstaining from liquor, pill, work, gambling, food, and sex addictions.

If hope is letting go of the attachment to the outcome of having it, why bother?

The mental gymnastics were exasperating. I dreamt I was lost, dazed and stumbling, aimless. Faltering and falling apart, shouting for help, unable to see. Blind to everything and keenly aware of the dark. I protested in one slumbering sideshow, "I don't wanna be in control."

Starving for any guideline scrap, I bought a crystal pendulum. The clerk at the healthy edibles and holistic healing store demonstrated how it would swing, back and forth, reacting to her command, "Show me Yes," and stopped after she said, "Stop." When she declared, "Show me No," the stone plumb bob at the end of a thin chain rotated in a wide circle.

"You can only ask questions about yourself. It can't give you answers for anyone besides you," she cautioned.

I shrewdly divined information concerning Captain. I paraphrased "Does Captain love me" to "Am I loved by Captain," reassured with a robust swing in the direction indicating "Yes." Rather than "Will Captain get sober" I asked, "Will I ever see Captain sober?" The result was consistently, "Nope."

Initially, the gadget provided reassurance and unscrambled conflicts. The information wound up as accurate as a Magic 8-ball, he-loves-me, he-loves-me-not daisy petals, mood rings, or those red cellophane fortune teller fish, curling, flopping, lying motionless, depending upon your hand's clamminess. The pendant's answers reported what I believed. Easily influenced truths; matters of illusionary fact. My faith fizzled. I fell back to flipping my Scottsdale "Resort Capital of Arizona" cowboy/roadrunner lucky souvenir coin for pointers. If the first toss was a disappointing cowboy, or I went for two-out-of-three roadrunners, my honest desire was apparent. If I didn't care about the result I abided by the flipped coin's direction. A primer for hope-less-ness.

*   *   *

My father joined a radio evangelical, cultish Christian religion that split our household into a take-no-prisoners war zone.

Christmas and Easter—pretty much all the traditional holidays except Thanksgiving—represented Pagan celebrations. He scrawled, "All Hallows Eve Paraphernalia" on the box storing pumpkin, ghost and goblin decorations, insinuating Halloween was satanic hoopla. I still get twinges that Pagan is synonymous with Lucifer.

His refusal to participate was annulled and his defiance denounced. On Christmas morning, I resented the Santa Claus deception as Dad, with his own beef, opened forced-upon presents. I savored shrimp wound with bacon and he scowled across the table. My reformed father maintained Old Testament Jewish dietary laws, traditions, and celebrations. Passover, matzoh bread, pork-less Feast of the Tabernacles, and how it all jumbled together with bible-thumping, Jesus lovin' Christianity was intriguing. He scampered to services on the "true" Sabbath—Saturday—and Mom hauled me off to the Lord's house on Sundays.

Dad rented a secure post office box and locked documents in a briefcase. He hid the key on account of Mom swiping correspondence from his church. Tithing thirty percent from his salary was as cataclysmic to the household finances as the annihilationist doctrine preached from the pulpit. Both parents dug in. They exemplified "What you resist, persists".

Tax evasion and other sundry sins blew the lid off The Worldwide Church of God, scandalizing the founding mastermind and his son. Dad limped to recognizing he had made a mistake. Months before his death he apologized for being wrong.

"It wasn't wrong, Dad," I said. "It was different." He had innocently kicked open the door to diversity.

My parents illustrated the futility in combating over who's right or wrong—above all, regarding the disease of religion. Turning to a church gave Dad a leg up to head off suffering. Nothing compared to Christ's tribulations; a consolation soothing the masses. Mom and Dad ultimately merged into a mutual congregation. The truce was pockmarked. Resentment steeped below the shallow surface of their marriage. They devolved into besting each other, becoming The Bickersons.

Sullied over my parents' vexed religious viewpoints, as an adult, I practiced devout avoidance through bitter obstinacy. Mom, the self-appointed Disciple For Lost Daughter's Salvation, accosted me with God's propaganda books. Never cracking the spines, I re-gifted the sneaky Christmas and birthday presents to churchy friends. Her relentless requests to attend worship rituals were met with "No thanks." Refusing became a principle. A single ask was a welcome; continuance was control.

In a mature attempt to be agreeable, I went with Mom to an Easter pageant performed near her Mesa, Arizona, home. I was curious if the Jesus story had any new plot twists. The Mormon Temple spectacle was a theatrical extravaganza with four hundred cast members, one hundred people backstage, and an ocean of audience. There were no reserved seats for the gala. We arrived hours before the opening curtain to ferret out a place to park the car and park our butts. Forty-five minutes before the introductory music, performers swarmed through the captive crowd, missionaries recruiting, shooting fish in a barrel. A young boy approached Mom and me.

"Is this your first time seeing the pageant?" he asked. Mom did the talking and I scrutinized the young'un. His costume was a graying white bed sheet, tied at the waist with a tawny rope. A matching rope and sheet swaddled his head.

"I was here with my husband a few years ago," Mom answered. I evaded eye contact.

"Where are you from?" he continued. The back-to-back inquiries were as much of the show's script as the spoken lines on the Goliath stage.

Demurring from describing herself as a lowly Arizona snowbird, Mom replied, "I'm a winter visitor and she's from Florida." I was now the target for the little shepherd's attention.

Before he angled his hustle in my direction, I jockeyed into the lead, quizzing, "What grade are you in?" He was in fifth grade. I went on interrogating the indoctrinated innocent.

"What's your favorite subject in school?"

"Is this your first pageant?"

"How do you like it?"

"What was the audition like?"

I paused between the shelling, giving him free rein to talk about himself.

"How many Jesuses are in the show?"

I struck twenty-four-carat gold.

He looked over his shoulder, making sure he wouldn't get busted for insurrection and said, "I think there's six. Maybe seven. There is a wet Jesus and a dry Jesus for the John the Baptist scene. After Jesus is baptized in the baby pool and is all wet, he rolls under the platform where you can't see, and then the dry Jesus is in the Palm Sunday scene. That's the next time you see Jesus."

"And one time," continuing to divulge secrets in breathless, fifth-grade boy exhilaration, "the donkey Jesus rode into Jerusalem on sat down and wouldn't move and Jesus got dumped."

The boy giggled. "Jesus had to walk off stage and they had to push the donkey on his rear end to get him to go."

"Cool," I said. It was showtime and my unsaved status was saved.

*   *   *

The steps to recovery are written as a cumulative string, the first flowing to the twelfth, and completing the steps in the sequence was strongly recommended. Step Three of the Twelve—turning my will and life over to the care of God—was a granddaddy tug-of-war to my isms: pragmatism, DIY-ism, agnosticism. An entire chapter in the *AA Big Book* is dedicated to discussing the agnostic. Apparently, I needed to trust in a major-league contender to conquer the program and not my cocky self. I had invested in four decades of dodging domination. Who knew better than me on how to run my life? Evidence from my struggles pointed to maybe I could use some help but acknowledging the Father, Son, and Holy Ghost, (a patriarchal authority three-pack), was a disagreeable horse pill to stomach. Abdicating self-rule would mean acquiescing to the original control freak.

With skepticism and wanting to believe about equal, I peeked across secular complacency looking for cynic-friendly, Higher Power proof. Recovering alcoholics who were able to tackle clean *and* sober demonstrated a vague, influential wellspring for their temperance and dignity. Drawn in by their grand slam, I began testing Supreme Being merits while holding out on total surrender.

I asked seasoned Twelve Stepper's hard questions. "What's the point of free will, God's glorious bounty, if, in keeping with Step Three, I'm supposed to turn my will over to God?" I never got a satisfying response.

Using Glinda's Bubble Theory (you possess the power) and applying Goldilocks' trial and error methodology, I sorted out answers for myself. If I am to do with this life, as I will, free to make choices, then the results are mine to willingly exploit. The converse is no less compulsory. Circumstance, without question, reflects judgment. Repeatedly making bad to worse choices is a dive down the rabbit hole to mayhem and insanity. Growing is better picking. Evolution is selective.

This fit. It jived with my aversion to puppet submissiveness. Free choice, as in self-governing rather than without cost, paired nicely with utilizing The Ten Commandments as a life path TripTik. A cause and effect travel planner with tangible suggestions and detours to avoid unpleasantness. "Thou shall not steal." "Thou shall not pass Go and collect $200." "Thou shall go directly to jail."

I reassessed "your will, not mine" and refashioned God - Allah - Great Spirit - Yahweh - Krishna - Gitchi Manitou - Lord Buddha - Divine Creator as directional arrows designating a mountaineering byway, pointing out an elevated evolution through wiser choosing. I had no problem praying for differential wisdom and the courage to be smarter. "How's that working for you?", a humorous way to chide Captain when he said, "I'm only drinking red wine from now on," also became my barometer for measuring blue ribbon and dud decisions.

Dispassionately accepting the deific direction hypothesis, I went on a quest for a bearable symbol. AA and Al-Anon provided a loophole, an amendment to Step Three. A generic God; *as we understand Him*. A higher power of my choosing. The Man Upstairs was wrong on so many levels. I had irrevocably unsubscribed to the literal interpretations of Dad's fundamentalist, and Mom's more traditional and passive-aggressive sin subversions and gravitated to a scientific superhuman, omnipotent explanation, joining the Higgs boson mass following. Subatomic God Particles created from a high-energy field, permeating space, contributing to the dynamism causing all matter interactions.

My parents were certain Eternal Life is an ever-lasting resurrected existence. The gates of heaven opened to the devoted who recognized Jesus as a paid-in-full voucher from human limitations and obeyed his consecrated rules. I hypothesized life eternal is an endless appetite for sentient beings; all animate life forms, to reproduce and exist. Not a thing; a process.

Overpopulating *Homo sapiens* are capable of ruining existence atop our rotating blue marble, Natural Law being what it is. Come what may, a primordial chowder nourished with pivotal ingredients—amino acids, saltwater, and energy supply—will assemble into microorganisms, copying themselves in a chain reaction buoyed by empowered get-up-and-go. Wiggling, thriving, multiplying, and evolving and advancing zing and *joie de vivre* through the Circle of Life. And what about galaxies, far far away? And parallel universes? Reincarnation? The weeds in my yard? Life tenaciously marches onward and upward.

Einstein's dream to discover the unified source of the diversified universe was essentially fulfilled by physic's Superstring Revolution. Hardly a deity I could snuggle up to for expressing gratitude or imploring guidance. Further muddling the metaphysical clutter, I had the idea life's supercharged energy is Love. Not the love holding me close at night, kissing me in the morning, the love I ached for, the kind that was stolen. I supposed big-L love could serve as a reminder that I am desirable, that everything is okay; will be okay. Cogitation gone wild made my skull feel like it was stuffed with cotton. Bottom line: either God is or God isn't. It didn't matter what I believed, as long as I mustered some form of faith. A process; not a thing. *Choose wisely, Grasshopper.*

*   *   *

If anything gives me pause to marvel, inspires awe, offers refuge, and a restful sanctuary for worship, it's Nature's virtue and stoic balance. Songbirds chirp hymns over the prayerful chant of monastic crickets. A stream's splashing sermon brings life and sustenance to all within its reach. Communion is an undisturbed walk in the woods. A kayak paddle to mangrove forests across diamond dotted water with a dolphin escort. Rest in soft grass beneath the sun's bear-hug warmth.

A cousin, who championed non-religious divinity, animal totems, and Reiki healing, lauded a comprehensive animal, bird, and reptile symbolism dictionary. The book added flash and dazzle to my embraceable theological metaphor and became a bible, contributing to my spiritual bloom. Peppered with torn papers signaling noteworthy pages and underlined text highlighting salient passages, it looked like Dad's battered *King James*, marked up and worn down.

Dragonflies buzzed by at dawn. A garden snake lounged in the afternoon heat. I spotted hermit, horseshoe, and spider crabs in the dimming evening light. After animal encounters, I consulted the book. I bumbled through interpretive scripture detailing the prehistory and meaning of their physical appearances. I meditated on the suggestions of what the animal could be teaching. Do I need to lighten up? Have I been too inflexible, resisting change? Do I trust my inner senses? Coming out of my shell? Am I trying to force things? Are others? Was I being shown to find joy and sing it out?

I resurrected the pendulum as a compass to identify personal animal essences. A "yes" motion denoted frogs and deer as my particular messengers. Their frequent comings and goings were hard to ignore.

"Yeah, well, frogs are plentiful in a tropical environment, and Key Deer reproduce safe and secure in a National Wildlife Refuge. They're everywhere! Of course, I see them all the time." I belittled my own dogma. The skittish tabby stared, awakened by my confessional outburst.

Recalling which came first—my recommitment to pursuing spirituality or confirmation my holy grail existed was an ageless chicken or egg conundrum. Either way, inspiring validations materialized like dandelions after a downpour.

Driving one very early morning through the hours stretching between starlight and sunrise, I hesitated at a four-way intersection. A traffic cop would call it a rolling stop. As the car moved forward, I heard a *thawump!* and slammed the brakes without slamming the clutch. The car lurched and stalled. A large blob blinked, perhaps winked at me through the windshield. According to Ted Andrews' *Animal Speak,* people with a frog spirit guide are reminded to use their voice to change the climatic conditions of their lives. I was, by then, fully engaged on the Al-Anon front line.

Frogs, a totem for metamorphosis, represent coming into one's creative power. Shamanic societies link the frog totem with water and controlling the weather. They counted on the amphibians to summon the rains. And the water element is associated with emotions. Semi-aquatic frogs promulgated their message from all over my yard. They adhered to window frames, sat tight under the hurricane shutters, and snuck into the house. Hopping reminders to think less, feel more, but don't drown in either pool.

*   *   *

Whenever Captain fell off their radar, his on-again, off-again employers, distanced sister, and anxious friends made their first investigative calls to me. Most often he was at my home, and I reassured them he was fine. These calls turned toward conversations on saving Captain. Plots for whisking him away to a mainland clinic jammed me into playing the weighty role of Judas. My misgivings escalated with each secret plan.

A perceptive, humorless Captain laid it on the line. Coercing recovery would end in disaster. Holding both my shoulders in a firm grip, he admonished, "Don't ever try to send me away, make me go to rehab. I will disappear and I promise you—you'll never see me again." The veracity of his dour testimony convinced me I was holding a one-way ticket across thin ice.

A sticky-toed tree frog, petite enough to fit in an espresso demitasse, hid behind a weatherproof painting hanging outside, between the window and the front door. The reliably present, abstract doorman came out from behind its refuge and perched atop the wooden picture frame in the course of a conniving phone call. Unaware of the observer, I leaned against the deck rail and talked with an intervention conspirator. Wedged between the desire—the hope—for Captain's chance at sobriety and forever losing him in the process, I sank under a load of what was and wasn't my responsibility. Regardless, I chose to give away detrimental information. The caller eagerly waited as I loosened the strings to spill the beans.

A smooth, damp, *splat!* on my face interrupted the briefing. A terrific yelp substituted the suspended words. Flapping my hands like a wet bird drying its wings, I gasped. "Oh! Yow! Oh! Omigod! A frog landed on my mouth!" I dropped the phone, the call, and all subsequent bids to recruit my assistance in Captain's business.

My bible says a frog defines its territory and calls out warnings of predators.

Science says when a belief is modified using cognitive reframing; the new thought pattern re-shapes brain function.

Spirit says, "I will appear to you as you see me."

If you ask to read me, assuming my spirit is just exotic
& cultured & non-threatening enough to be within

the many magics you believe are your own, I am flattered
by the half-right assumption; that my knowledge of crystals

goes past rock & pipe. I'm sorry too, because the things
in my pocket are just junk. These coins are not tokens.

I don't know how to throw bones. I'm just too shy to litter
& now I'm in a room with glazed rocks & matches

that look too expensive to be lit. I can't tell if we believe
in spirits or if we perform with things but I hope

we haven't assigned spirits to the things in this room
because everything in here makes me uneasy.

I take no joy in inflating prices for dead & sacred plants
or funding factory bones, separated from creatures to throw.

My dad told me of tree ogres, horse heads smoking cigarettes,
& bat harpies who could eat my entrails. I am still

terrified of all of them. Every year, I bang pots & spatulas
to scare away whatever demons exist in this country. You

don't get to call me a skeptic. I don't want to hear
what the stars have in store for me. All I hear every day

are what the senators & priests & police & landlords & academics
have in store for me. Just like the laws, the stars seem

to only protect a certain class of people. Consulting birth charts;
results of a mystic census polled from the greater universe

delivered by a speaker I do not know. No more.
I'm tired of experts narrating my lifespan.

Girolamo, a gray-bearded, studious man of forty-six, sat at his inclined wooden desk against the forward wall of the captain's quarters. He dipped his quill in the inkwell and squinted at the map, carefully shading the tip of Cape Fear, from which Le Dauphine was preparing to disembark. The rains of late winter lashed at the window behind him, falling out of a gray sky that the skipper, his younger brother, had decided to ignore and set sail. Above him, on the poop deck, he heard a sudden clutter of footsteps, voices, and laughter. The heavy clunk of his brother's footsteps approaching followed shortly after, and Giovanni soon burst into the room. He was three years his brother's junior, with a stringy black beard spliced into two braids and bushy eyebrows that lent him a predatory, rapturous scowl. He breathed heavily and looked around.

"Giro." he said, panting, "Come to the deck! I have to show you something."

Girolamo stood slowly, wrapped his pelt cloak around his shoulders, and followed Giovanni up the steps. The two men bumped their shoulders against the walls of the narrow stairway with each gentle toss of the boat. At the top of the steps, Giovanni whipped aside the tapestry, and Giro shaded his eyes with his hands against the midmorning winter sky.

About half of the fifty-man crew was crowded together on the main deck with their backs turned to the two brothers. They were staring at something at the base of the mainmast.

The crew was comprised mostly of Frenchmen but contained a motley assortment of others. There were Florentine noblemen, seeking fortune in the New World but possessing no useful nautical skills, but helped fund the endeavor and were allowed to tag along. A few Berber expatriates served as mercenaries, but only after being converted and receiving Communion. Three Catholic priests from Marseille were aboard, mostly to educate and convert the Indians. Girolamo had complimented one of them on the ornate crucifix he wore; a tall, lanky man with no hair at all named Taulet. The crucifix was beset with sapphire and made of white gold. Taulet had grinned at Girolamo, reached inside his frock, and pulled out another necklace, upon which dangled a blackened and shriveled human tongue. The priest explained he had cut it from the mouth of a Huguenot during a rebellion ten years prior to refusing the host.

"Did he die?" Girolamo had asked.

"She most probably did," the priest shrugged.

Girolamo followed as Giovanni pushed through the crowd up to the mast. Upon the quarter-deck, an archer of Timurid stock, who represented the crewman from the furthest inland, laughed and clapped, his toothless mouth yawning in a wide, malevolent grin.

Against the mast, cowering against the glares of dangerous men and the cold, crouched a little native boy about eight. He was dressed only in a loincloth and had a small black pelt wrapped around his shoulders. He shivered and wiped raindrops from his forehead, staring back at the group.

"What do you think, Giro?" Giovanni asked. "I coaxed him onboard with bits of fried dough and brown sugar. What should we use him for?"

Giro considered the child. He was slightly larger than an Italian child of his age would be. His slender legs appeared suited to running long distances. His shoulders and chest were ropy, small threads of sinew twisting themselves through each other under goose-bumped skin. He was slim, but he seemed athletic. His skin was the color of red clay and possessed a face that featured prominent cheekbones and jet-black irises smoldered like coals. The boy's hair was smooth and silken, and braided into two pigtails that ran down his long back.

Giovanni pulled from his heavy scarlet robe a piece of dough. The child stared back at him for a moment, then reached out and snatched it. The child turned it over in his hands, studying it, then looked back at Giovanni. Giovanni pointed his hand to his own mouth as he opened and closed it. The child took a bite from the piece of dough, and the ghost of a smile crossed his face as he chewed.

"I almost had a girl, too," Giovanni told his brother. "I grabbed her by the neck, but she started screaming and elbowed me in the gut, so I just grabbed the kid and got out of there."

"Has he said anything?" Girolamo asked. He paused, took off his pelt cloak, and went to put it over the child, but the child winced and crept further around the mast, out of Girolamo's reach. "What about that translator? Can he get us the kid's name?"

"I don't think the translator is in a condition to do anything, but we can try."

Girolamo looked over the port side of the ship at a flat stretch of sandy beach across the choppy water. They were close enough that someone could reach land alone in a rowboat in about ten minutes, but might freeze if they tried to swim it. Off in the hazy distance, he could make out a tree line behind the beach. He wondered how many other children like this one we're living in the forest across the water.

*   *   *

Blue Turtle finally gave in to the cold and crawled under the pelt. He hid his head under it, afraid to look out at the large men standing around him. He could hear the men talking and laughing as he ate the morsel that the most strangely dressed of the pale faces had given him. What would he do now? What would they do to him next? He rubbed his father's scalp that sat on his shoulders against his cheek.

A hand lifted the blanket off of Blue Turtle's head. Blue Turtle looked up to see a pale face grinning back at him and holding his hand out. The man had some sort of black cover over one of his eyes, and said something in his language, holding his hand closer. In the man's hand was an orange disc, as small as a seashell, which Blue Turtle accepted and sniffed. The aroma was pleasant, like citrus. He placed it in his mouth and attempted to bite down, but it was hard and hurt his teeth. Blue Turtle sucked on it for a moment, enjoying the flavor, as another man stepped over and kicked him in the ribs. He spit the candy onto the deck. The man who had given it to him pushed the one who had kicked Blue Turtle away, as the boy ducked back under the cloak.

An hour ago he had been wandering the shoreline, face turned up to catch the raindrops, making up songs in his head.

*   *   *

Giovanni pushed a pile of maps Girolamo had made off to the side of his desk and pulled out a cask of red wine and two glasses. He filled each of them.

"What are we to do with the kid?" Girolamo asked.

"I was hoping you could think of something," Giovanni said. "We could always use another pair of hands."

"And another mouth?" Girolamo said, sipping his wine. "We've been eating slop every day for the past few weeks, and now Pierre's got to feed our new charge."

Giovanni sat down in his chair and turned to stare at the sky through the window behind him. The raindrops hitting the pane of glass tapered off a bit as Giovanni sipped his wine. "Well, he's a curiosity, anyway," he said. "Most of the crew has never seen anything like him."

It was true. Aside from the two brothers and the three priests, only a few of the crewmembers had set foot on the solid ground of the New World. Some parts were more hospitable than others; the Timurid had taken a small arrow to the shoulder in a forest some three weeks prior. He had killed the man who shot him and fled to the boat, having learned archery skills on the steppes of Central Asia. Girolamo was impressed by how easily such skills had transferred to forest terrain. That had been the Timurid's only contact with the locals on their own turf, and he had not stuck around to get a closer look.

"He is a curiosity alright," Girolamo said.

"Bring him to the hold," Giovanni said. "We'll see if that poor bastard down there can tell us anything."

*   *   *

The pale face led Blue Turtle to the bottom of the massive ship. Blue Turtle didn't know ships this big existed; it was like a city in the water. The boy held his hands out to steady himself against the walls with each throe of the tide as they walked into the darkest bowels of the vessel. Eventually, they came to a small room cast in dim sunlight by two small holes on either wall.

The passageway they traversed now was just as narrow, but there were iron bars on either side. In one of these cages, a man lay on the floor. The pale face called out to him. The man barely stirred. The pale face opened the lower section of the iron gate and slid a bucket of freshwater through, then called out to the man again.

Blue Turtle watched as the man slowly rolled over and crawled to the bucket. The man wheezed and groaned, as he was barely able to move, and when the pale face asked him something in his own language, the man looked up at Blue Turtle.

The man was covered in oozing sores. His eyelids were completely scabbed over, and his bloodshot eyes leaked pus that ran down his face and dripped to the floor like spring water from a mountainside. The man attempted to pull his face up to the rim of the bucket and open his bloody mouth for a sip of water, but he upset the bucket and spilled half the water before the pale face reopened the gate and set the bucket upright.

Blue Turtle took a step backward and hid behind the pale face as the man drank greedily from the bucket. After two gulps, he coughed and sputtered, spitting water back onto the wooden floor. The pale face spoke to the man on the floor. As the pale face continued to speak, the man wretched and vomited a small string of yellow fluid into the growing puddle beneath him. When the pale face stopped speaking, the man looked up at Blue Turtle, and Blue Turtle shrank again.

"Child," the man wheezed. "What is your name?"

"Blue Turtle."

"And where are you from?"

"Quiripi, in the Dawnland."

"Ha. I am from the Dawnland too." He rolled over and scratched at the suppurating sores on his chest and a cascade of bloody fluid poured down his torso. "I am Abenaki."

The child lurched forward and grabbed the bars of the cage. He held his hand out and stroked the side of Abenaki's head as he asked him another question.

The pale face said something to the man, and the man laid his face down on the floor and said something back in the pale face's own language. There was silence for a moment, and the pale face kicked the bars of the cage. The man did not move.

*   *   *

The next day was warm and the water was calm. Giovanni had Le Dauphine anchored offshore of the channel that would someday be named for him, and he sent two crewmen and Taulet, the priest, down into a dinghy with fishnets. The men hauled a few nets full of cod from the chilly, glimmering midmorning surf.

Blue Turtle sat with his back against the mainmast, coiling a length of rope, as Girolamo had shown him. He listened to the shouts of the fishing crew members, and they all sounded to be in high spirits. The child ruminated on the man in the hold. The image of the festering sores on his body had haunted the boy all night.

There was a sudden thrashing in the water midway between the ship and the dinghy. Blue Turtle peeked over the deck. A pod of six harbor porpoises was circling the craft, occasionally breaching and spraying the laughing sailors from their blowholes.

Blue Turtle stood on the railing, took a quick glance at Girolamo, and dove headfirst into the surf.

The water was frigid. Blue Turtle swam underwater towards the porpoises. He came up for breath no more than a man's length from the dinghy, reached out, and grabbed hold of the first dorsal fin that came near. The animal immediately dove under, and Blue Turtle hitched a ride, gliding through a Mesmer where there was no time or law, just he and this denizen of Atlantis living a small life together in all of a moment. When the animal had swum halfway to the seafloor, Blue Turtle let go of the fin and swam toward the surface, exhaling an exhaust of bubbles. He popped his head back up into the air and pulled his hair out of his eyes to see another porpoise leap from the water just behind the dinghy. The three crewmen were laughing at the boy, and Taulet stood up in the boat applauding while trying to keep his balance.

Blue Turtle swam up to the dinghy and trod water as the porpoises lost interest and swam off. One of the crewmembers beckoned to him to get into the boat, and Blue Turtle went underwater again and swam under the bottom of the boat. He came up on the other side with a mouthful of water bulging his cheeks. The men in the rowboat turned and he spat a stream of water at them. The men laughed at this, and the man with the eye patch threw the empty fishing net over the boy and yanked him up out of the water and into the boat.

*   *   *

Girolamo stood on the deck that night. The moon overhead was almost full, and the reflection on the surface of the water was like a celestial carpet leading the way to the shores of the New World. He had eaten a heaping portion of the day's catch, and now most of the men were in bed while the ship remained anchored. Girolamo knew the Timurid archer was sitting watch in the crow's nest, but all was silent. The men on the deck dozed in heaps. He walked with his hands clasped behind his back, towards the stern, all the while scanning the shoreline for signs of life or movement. As he walked past the mainmast, he saw Blue Turtle sleeping on a coil of rope, beneath the fur cloak he had been given.

He stood over the child. He turned to look at the shore again, so close he could make out each individual tree. He looked up at the moon, hanging in the sky, watching over all of them like a mother

Girolamo stooped down. He picked up the slumbering child under the armpits. The boy stirred but did not make a sound. Girolamo turned around and threw him into the water.

RC DEWINTER
SECOND SKIN

there's nothing quite like

the fitting of one's skin over that of another
and finding you wear the same shadow
dusted with the fine particulate matter of your souls

a grounding of such enormity that once discovered
creates the necessity of the other as a condition of existence

you can call it love but that shopworn word
the property of hucksters selling everything

from flowers to secondhand cars
doesn't begin to describe the overlayment of the other

on what you now realize was only half
of what life was meant to be

this cat was called Champagne Sam   and he came when granddad died
    in the summer   and his corpse   swelled up   melon ripe and velvet soft

Sam likes to eat grass and   lingers where fevers do He likes to stick
his whiskers   into scorpion's eyes   He is too   fast for
                                                   their tails to catch

granddad   taught us the way to skin cats   but not
what to do once their skin   is limp   and warm
            and wet in   our hands

you don't keep a cat's pelt for sport,   not

unless he never sinned,   and every cat is a sinner

we skinned cats that cheated for extra lives after their nine
tucked our   scalpels gently so   beneath the seam
on the belly   and pulled

we ribcage and salt the unsettled bones   for hanging on the porch,

or rattling in   ma's little   bottles

but no one's touched granddad's cat blade since   before he went and tied a

                     knot to his vena cava

and his headstone starts to   groan loud enough   to hear
from up the road   when someone gets
                              close enough to try

WOMANHOOD

A dollop of moonshine to the wound,
rustic remedy to mend a crumbling muscle.
My sister peels back my skin to reveal pulsations
that have been out of sync since I turned ten.
She touches my cheek, whispers, "It hurts,"
but she does not know why.

He does not believe me when I tell him.
Words fight through yellowed teeth, his
countered digestion, "That means we can't—"
I sit at the edge of his bed and sigh.
Finally, my body has produced a weapon
valiant enough to fend off his sexual hunger,
an appetite I was forced to feed since I was seven.

My mother opens the green, square-shaped package,
the sounds of plastic balanced by the texture
of clouds. She instructs me how to use the wings,
fold here, press there. "Blood may leak," she warns.
I want to tell her that I have bled there before,
many times, but I nod and repeat her steps.

There are holes in my stomach, bulleted
and punched. Now that I was no longer his toy,
family visits weighed less. I was not shedding
the outer layer of my body anymore.
The morning he did not look at me during breakfast,
that was when I knew. I had finally won.

I'm in my hotel bed in Rome, alone, as I've been for five days straight. I'm holding a knife in my hands and my heart is beating fast. I've just heard a noise.

The knife is stolen, obviously, because you can't bring a knife on a plane, and I've just come from Bologna, where I spent four months becoming the type of person who would steal a steak knife from a restaurant because she thinks someone has been sneaking into her hotel room.

My reasoning for believing this is as follows: earlier today, I bought a new, bright blue cardigan. It was *exactly* what I wanted—the perfect shade of blue, so that people seeing it would remember that my eyes are blue, and child-sized so that it wouldn't bunch up around my waist when I wore it with my high rise jeans. I got back to the hotel and put on the cardigan immediately, taking off my shirt because I wanted it to touch my skin. (So soft.) I went downstairs to the lobby, left the hotel for dinner, then came right back to my tiny, tiny room. The sweater returned with me to the room—it *had* to return with me to the room, right? I wasn't wearing anything underneath it—where I disrobed to get in the shower. And then, incredibly, unmistakably, when I got out of the shower, the sweater was no longer there.

I searched for hours, believe me. It wasn't there. The only time when it could have disappeared? *While I was in the shower.*

I'm trying to slow my heart rate by thinking it all through rationally, but the facts just don't add up to a comforting reality. Of all things to take, my *cardigan?* If my imagined breaker-and-enterer had stolen my computer, which was left out in the open, or my passport, which was somewhat concealed in a backpack pocket, that would certainly have been upsetting—emergency passports are costly, and new Macs are costlier—but a cardigan is different. Stealing a sweater is an intimate act. When you pass up the computer in order to take the cardigan, you have a more sinister intent than theft at heart.

I've just heard the noise again. It sounds like someone very, very close to me is getting a text. My phone only vibrates once with each text I receive, but this is a two-buzz notification, and it has happened thrice in the past 15 minutes, and *no one* is communicating with me right now.

The mystery man who's *so* enamored with me that he stole my brand new sweater (and is now lying beneath my bed receiving text messages) could only be someone with a key to the room, I think. My door only has a regular lock—no night lock. So the mystery man has to be someone with access to my room key, someone who works at the hotel.

It also has to be a man, without a doubt. I've met enough men in the past four months to know that. I used to think that humans were intrinsically good; I believed that we all had the capacity to love and be loved and that the people who got arrested for crimes had just strayed from the path. Now I think a man is hiding underneath my bed, waiting for me to go to sleep so that he can slit my throat and then have sex with my corpse.

I don't blame living abroad for this change. You can probably live abroad and not develop a hatred of men, but that's not what happened to me. I was warned about Italian men before I left America, but I didn't care—I'd lived in New York City my whole life, I *knew* street harassment. When men holler at you while you walk down the street, it's unpleasant but ignorable. They're not doing anything that bad, really, just talking, just making conversation. But when they *touch* you? When it's a nice day out, so you wear a strapless shirt with butterflies on it, and a man grazes your arm with his hand and whispers in your ear, "Ooh girl, let me just suck on your titties"? When a boy tries to smack you on the ass, and then he finds your responsive shriek so charming that he chases you for a full block, laughing uproariously at a joke you maybe didn't hear? When it's your birthday and an ancient man cups your buttock in one hand and croons something you don't understand that makes you shiver despite the humidity of the Bolognese fall? It becomes hard not to start hating something.

The most confusing element of my current predicament is that I'm not even sexy. Sure, I'm tall and skinny, and once a kid in tenth grade congratulated me on the fact that my boobs were "the melons," but no one has ever used the word "hot" to describe me. So at first, it was flattering to be here, where all I have to do is smile at a man to get him to slip me his number on a crumpled up napkin as I stand up to leave. "This is yours." "Venga di nuovo, signorina." It felt like being beautiful. One night, I was feeling bold and decided to post my Instagram username on my Tinder profile, and I got 40 likes, 12 followers, 10 DMs, and two dick pics (of two separate dicks!) while I slept off the alcohol. One of them was from a soccer player with a pretty big following. I thought it made me powerful, that I could inspire that type of reaction; now I know better.

Who could be under the bed right now? Let's guess. Shouldn't be hard: I've only seen three hotel employees since I arrived, one of whom was a woman, and one of whom I met for the first time when I returned from dinner only a few hours ago, so it wouldn't make sense for him to already be so obsessed with me to warrant stealing my clothing to create a life-size, me-shaped sex robot (unless there is surveillance technology installed in my bedroom?). It has to be the other man, the one who was working at reception when I checked in and was *so* impressed that I could respond to his questions in both Italian and English.

Yeah, now that I think of it, he *must* be the one. I'm kind of surprised because he didn't seem that aggressive when I met him, at least not as some other men do. Perhaps his indifferent gaze and blank smile were just a mask for how he really felt, which was lustful and murderous. He certainly looks the part of a self-proclaimed incel. He's long and emaciated—skinny enough to be currently hiding under my bed, for sure. He gave me free Prosecco two nights ago and asked me for my name to tag me in something on Facebook, and when I hesitated he insisted that he had a wife and children, so it was okay. "Don't worry, I have a wife! Ho dei figli!" Did he protest too much? I didn't think so at the time, but now I'm thanking every instinct in my still-breathing body that I didn't tell him who I was. Even though I bet he could find it out easily anyway because he runs the hotel. He probably has, since then. Maybe he's looking through my profile pictures at this very instant, two feet below me.

It would be strange for this "happily married" man to try to kill me *now*, though, because he already had the perfect opportunity. He could've easily put something in my Prosecco, and by this time my seizures would be long done, my frothed spit already wiped clean from my little mouth, my blue cardigan already returned lovingly to my frozen, blue body. Though now that I think about it, there were two French women in the room with us when he gave me the Prosecco, so maybe he didn't poison me then because he didn't want any witnesses? Or maybe the thrill of the physical kill is what really appeals to him? Maybe the thought of my body, formerly wrapped up in my darling blue cardigan like a present, torn limb from limb and used as a paintbrush to render a portrait across the comforter is what really gets him off? Who knows. All I know is that if I fall asleep, I might never wake up, so I'm stuck lying here awake until 9 am, when I get to leave this cheap hotel room and never come back to Italy.

I didn't meet a single redeemable man here. Maybe they exist, but I didn't meet them. Instead, I met the man who hollered "E' arrivata la pussy"—"The pussy has arrived"—as I walked by. I met the man who followed me on his bike very slowly as I walked to class three days in a row. I met the man who stood in the center of a portico and tried to grab every woman who walked past around the waist. I met the group of men who tried to talk to my friends, and me and after they were rejected, followed us through the streets of Florence for ten minutes and rang the doorbell to our apartment for ten more. I met the man who recognized my friend from a picture he had taken in a club of her making out with another woman two weeks previously and showed it to me, and when I got upset, whispered in my ear that he was going to go home and masturbate to the photo.

And then I met the two men in the black turtlenecks that help me stay willfully awake for fear of nightmares. The men who saw me stranded in the club, alone like I am now, and reached out. Intoxicated, tripping my way unprotected to the bathroom without my friends, I thought they were friendly—so when the first man grabbed my hand and pulled me in to dance, I danced. I was too drunk at first to notice that the other man stood too close on the other side, two walls trapping me in; and then I didn't know how to resist when they held my body steady and twisted my face from one of their tongues to the other, for minutes, while they toured my body with their shameful fingers. I dream often about their saliva all over me, the slime trails left by two slugs, my body defiled. My skin is sticky still; I shower for hours.

That's how the bastard got my cardigan out of my room, I'm sure. I showered for so long. He could've snuck in and out of my room ten times. He could've planted a bomb. He could've rubbed his tiny penis on every single surface. He could've stolen more stuff, stuff I haven't noticed yet—dirty underwear, maybe. I need to check my laundry. Why haven't I checked my laundry yet? Stupid. It's almost like I'm playing directly into his hands, those awful hands that will creep around my neck before the sun rises.

I asked the director of my program, after I met the turtlenecked men, whether I could talk to an English-speaking therapist. He closed the door and gave me tissues and told me he was there to listen, and that the only English-speaking therapist the program recommended was a man. I got the therapist's contact information from him and I left and I didn't call the therapist.

It's being alone, I think, that is the problem. I wouldn't feel this way if I weren't alone right now. When you're alone, every street corner has a man right around it, every window shade could be hiding a man's body, every queen size bed has a man-from-the-front-desk-who-*definitely*-has-a-family lying down and texting underneath.

There's the noise again. *Buzz buzz.* I grip my stolen knife tight.

On some level, I know I won't need to use it. I know there's no man under my bed. This man I've imagined doesn't exist, so he *can't* have my perfect blue sweater tucked into his bedside table, right next to all the photos he took of me naked in the shower. There are no cameras in the bathroom vent or the corners. All my dirty underwear is still with the rest of my dirty laundry. The wall at the back of the closet isn't fake, and it certainly doesn't lead to a secret dungeon replete with dentist tools and jars filled with eyeballs and olives. I know there's no man under my bed, waiting diligently for me to fall asleep so that he can ruin me more than I already have been. But I'm still holding a knife right now. Can you blame me?

i used to tell people you were dead, it was easier than the shape of your mouth
when you said no –
tragic accident
a fellowship in another state.
i used to wish you were dead,
hated the way my heart worked hard
and moved my blood from one end of the room to another.
will you live here when you're older? green as a snake
i used to hope you would disappear
so i could miss you. the relief
of grief

i used to question your death
your reality tentative, sweltering
the cool insanity of that blue room

what you should know is my heart lives on that awkward avenue
on the third floor, i know where you are
at any given time
a bubble of cruelty
that cold mean kindness
pitiless
as smoke.
what you should know is i meant it, it would have easier
if you had never come back
i would not have stopped feeling
but i might have forgotten the gasp of you in a room

what you have to understand is we are all complicit
and it is as much my fault
as yours

For two years. I was abused.

I had my life. Stolen from me. By a woman who thought that it was hers for the taking.

She told me she loved me. And I believed her. She...Told me she'd "give me the world", but instead she made me not want to be a part of it.

Anymore.

She was a narcissist. That's what they do. That's what I lived with. And, I don't talk much about it, because...there's the cliché. The eye roll when you start talking about abuse from some idiot that thinks I'm just the bitter ex.

And I know I'm just another one, in a long line of...other ones...but when I do, when I do talk about it, I find people don't. Really know... What a narcissist is? What it means?

People seem to think it's this, "self obsessed, delusions of grandeur"...way of being. But it's not. It's...worse than that. It's more.

It's like being suffocated, only you're letting it happen. Because you just don't have enough energy left to fight to live.

I used to watch *Last Tango* in Halifax. It sounds silly, but there was this character on it. In it. Gillian - I was like Gillian. I was...self-destructive. I felt like I knew her - I identified with her. I connected with her when I didn't have anyone else; she'd stopped me from seeing my friends. She stopped me from seeing my family.

I talked to her in my head. Gillian. I'd imagine her walking next to me. So I could get from A to B without falling apart.

That made me feel even crazier.

It's hard to talk about what happened during that time. It's hard to say it out loud.

I didn't notice it in the beginning. Everything we did was her idea. Everything was...done on her terms.

I suppose that should have been a sign.

I was gaslit. That's another one of those terms that a lot of people don't really get. And I didn't really know it. Didn't know it at all, actually, until a friend pointed it out, and even then I didn't believe her, and I hated myself for believing the cliché that *she might get better.*

She would change situations, events, things I, or we, had done or said, and she would retell them in such a convincing way, that I would second-guess my memories. And gradually, gradually, I would tell myself I was wrong. And I would believe what she said was true. What actually happened.

She was in a position of power. She had a good job. People respected her and people believed her, so why shouldn't I trust her?

That's how she ended up making me clean and tidy her house everyday. She told her mum that I was so good at tidying. So good at looking after the house whilst she was at work.

She wrote me job lists every single day. Here, I'll show you one:

1- Can you give both fridges (Little one in garage and kitchen one) an anti-bac out. Not a long job, but just get them cleaner.

2- Can you throw out the out of date food?

3- Can you locate grey covered iPad?

4- Can you change all bed sheets?

5- Open windows to let the fresh air in.

6- Wash and hang out the rugs

7- Clear the entrance to the garage/fridge side a little

8- Check the dogs for fleas.

9- Hoover, clean, dust and general tidy whole house

10- Do laundry.

But that's not half of it. That's not even the tip of the iceberg.

In the time that I spent with her, I stopped writing. I stopped drawing. I couldn't write because I didn't have time, and I couldn't draw because my hands shook.

I wasn't earning any money.

I ran out of money.

I ran out of time.

She bullied me. Humiliated me. Belittled me in private and in front of...anyone. Everyone.

She raped me

But how do you...how do you prove that? People are often surprised, even doctors. Medical professionals. When they hear of a woman raping another woman.

They doubt it.

How could sex between two women be violent enough to cause physical or mental pain or injury? How was it rape if I never said no?

She cheated on me...too. Several times. More than once. More than I know. With...three women. There was one. Sarah. Right from the very beginning. We were kept apart, never allowed to meet, or talk, or...

There were other women. She'd hide her phone from me; tilted the screen away so I couldn't catch a glimpse of a name or a message.

Once, I managed to look through her phone. We were at the beach, and I went back to get something. To the car. I saw her phone on the seat, and I looked at it.

She called me paranoid.

I called it intuition. It was worth the silent treatment.

I read a few messages, but I didn't have time to read them all. There were so many lies, about me, about her, about her life.

And what shocked me the most was that she lied about things just to make me out to be a bad partner. A bad person. She made me out to be this...monster. This person she could barely stand to be around, who didn't buy her enough gifts, didn't *put her first* or make her, *top of their list.*

And I know. She will tell so many people the same stories she told me about her ex. She will cry and tell them all how she is the victim.

She will tell them how I reacted, but she won't tell them what she did to cause it.

I was scared. I was lonely. I lived in a fight or flight response. Always ready to apologise, make better, or diffuse a situation by immediate defeat. I had become a non-person. I was afraid to reach out for help for the same reason I was afraid to leave. Because I was terrified of the consequences and her reaction if she found out.

I was dead before I realised I was dying

*   *   *

These words I have spoken over the last ten minutes?

They're not mine.

I stole them. All of them. From the woman I told I loved.

It was easy.

And that's how I did it.

That's how I killed her.

QUINCY CRANE
THE FMK

And he's pressing against me
my mother taught me to always smile always
be nice, be happy, or else *no* one will like you
I was the butt of schoolboy jokes
...Fuck no! She's for sure a murder...
there were the baby steps in school
then the flood
a weighted definition
you are Woman
after sex-sectioned off health classes
those boys' eyes change
my best friend was full of shame
he looked away turning to his new friends
One-of-the-boys to start in with
jokes about womanhood
then later leaving home
leaving youth leaving
the ugly face of puberty leaving those
solemn, saddened eyes of teachers named
Ms. and Mrs. those
hungry glances from the men you called Mr.
you no longer see shame in the eyes of a man
they're grown, they'll never feel shame again
their eyes are shaded, dark with
power
vengeance
you are Woman
backing into a dark corner
I'd said *no, I said*
NO
but I was scared and couldn't enforce it
I was taught to be a *lady*
and ladies aren't woman enough to be hated
he's smiling and I'm shaking because
I know the game that he's playing
I guess I'd fuck her but she's more of a kill than a marry.

my fingers smell like nicotine.
not the good kind.
the good kind comes from my mother
who smokes out her nose like the dragons
from the chinese buffets
we liked to eat at on sundays.

we have been so careless about love.
careless is the word to use because
the good kind of love is not careless.
it wraps you up and holds you so close
smoke starts coming out of your nose.

we are both women just looking
for a little something to fill us up.

A draining six hours passed. Mercy was sanctioned when the clock struck 2 am. At last, my manager permitted me to leave his whorehouse. A few too many of my coworkers and I crammed ourselves into the small bathroom to change. Unclasping my silver high heels in the bathroom gave me the amount of pleasure I'd pretend to experience during a transaction with a client. Lines of cocaine were snorted off the sink through someone's $20 bill while we changed from our lingerie into sweatpants and hoodies. I jammed a few hundred dollars into the side of one of my boots. I shoved my cards into the side of my other boot. My phone and house keys were placed into a discreet inner pocket in my denim jacket. In one of the outer pockets, I kept a knife for protection and a $20 bill in case I wanted food. The other outer pocket on my jacket contained two pepper sprays. I used a reusable grocery store bag to transport my lingerie. I was smarter than to put anything valuable in it on the likely chance I got robbed.

I finished changing with my coworkers and hugged them all goodbye. A surplus of cheap wine and vodka sat on a glossy, black marble countertop in the kitchen corner of the renovated house my manager currently ran his business out of. I poured myself one last drink of vodka and ginger ale into a red Solo cup. I decompressed from my night on one of the black leather futons in the main room. Throughout my shift, I had downed a careless amount of alcohol and cocaine into my system. While I sipped on my last drink I scavenged through my surviving flashes of memory. I knew I had performed multiple sessions, but Samuel was the only specific face I recalled having sex with. On second thought, the face may have belonged to his brother Robert. Whatever. Miniscule details like who had sex with me or who didn't have stopped mattering.

Throughout my first year working under my manager, I got away with not having sex with any of my clients. Any kind of sexual favor a man could dare to dream up was allowed on the bargaining table except for (good ol' fashioned) sex. I liked feeling in control of my limitations somehow. However, fewer limitations promised more money and a better status with my manager. Luckily, he considered me one of his favorite girls so he acted easily on me. Even though I was one of his main bitches, I was still his bitch and I never forgot that. Constantly feeling different pairs of wicked hands tugging savagely at every inch of my pretty skin was a type of exhaustion deserving of its own category. Maybe I could work a real job instead, but that'd be ignorant; I no longer was naive enough to believe my existence held a purpose beyond men taking whatever gratification they needed from me, whenever they commanded. My existence belongs to men and the hands they couldn't keep off of me.

After I finished my drink, I slung my bag onto my shoulder, peeled myself off of the futon, and headed to the exit. On my way out I hugged my manager goodbye. Another night complete. In my wildest dreams, maybe this time, I'd disappear forever. The outside air felt refreshing against my skin and helped me to feel slightly more human after doing all those sinful things I'll take to my grave. I ventured deep into the darkness towards the El Train.

As I headed towards the stop, I made extra sure to keep up a swift walking pace, my eyesight in a steady 360-degree rotation, and hands in my pockets clenching my weapons. By this point I had mapped out everywhere I might obtain refuge should a strange man or car start following me. Location number one was to my left, a dive bar. Usually, people stood waiting outside for Uber at this hour. A few blocks up to my right was a house that typically blasted music late into the morning. Friendly-looking Christmas lights decorated the house despite Christmas not being close at all. For some reason this made me trust whoever lived inside. The last location I kept note of, and likely the most reliable resource for potential help, was the late hour's Chinese food shop about half a block away.

I made it to the entrance of the El Train station. Instead of stumbling up the subway steps and clumsily hopping over the turnstile to avoid paying my subway fare per usual, my feet stopped dead in my tracks. The lurking, sinister presence I often sensed in this area dotted goosebumps down my neck. My head twisted to the right. My grieving, brown eyes rested upon the late hour's Chinese food shop. A faint glow radiated off the red and yellow sign. Within the triangular frame of the glow, I noticed him lingering.

Don't ask me why I did it. I don't know the "why". Maybe it was the fault of the cocaine or the alcohol or having sex with weird men for money or carrying enough traumas to satisfy another few lifetimes. Maybe it was because college is hard or the depression or the ADHD or maybe it was because I was having trouble sleeping with myself. One thing I do know is that it would be unfair of me to pin the blame on a single reason alone or absolve myself from being a primary source of the blame. With drunken confidence and an unmatched recklessness, I walked directly up to the man.

"Do you know anyone who's selling around here?" I asked. He nodded and invited me to follow him. I felt hesitant but my determination to acquire what I found desiring felt overwhelming for me to divide any attention towards my better judgment.

His voice sounded distinctly deep. His stature and demeanor were just as intimidating as you would imagine. On a good day, I stand barely 5'2" tall. He towered above so tremendously that I needed to tilt my head upward to make eye contact. I trusted he understood his role in my fate wasn't to cause death; it was to guide me to it.

"Don't worry, we're not going far," he reassured me. "Would you like a cigarette?" Without saying a word, I took the cigarette and watched him light it between my pretty lips stained with faded red lipstick. Consoling me with a cigarette was an awfully courteous deed. His dark eyes contained undertones of sympathy in them. Above, I heard the deep clanking and then metallic screeching from the El Train tracks as the usual train I'd take home pulled up, then left.

"Just make sure to give me a few drags because it's my only one...You know I can tell you're not from around here," he said.

"Yea, it's been a minute since I've been down here," I said. That wasn't a lie. It *had* been a while since I hung around here. However, I had only ever indulged in daytime experiences. Now it was nighttime;

things shift from perilous to evil. Being anything but alone out here is a vulnerable illusion.

"What gave it away?" I asked.

"You seem nervous, " he said. This felt unfair to call me out on. Surely everyone's a little afraid to die. "You also look like you must be straight out of high school."

"Yea just about," I said. That was a lie. I was older. Correcting him seemed useless. With very few drags left to inhale I remembered to pass the cigarette over.

Ten minutes into our walk we reached the point of no return. He guided me through a shadowy alleyway behind a row of houses. We halted at a wooden backdoor of one of the houses. An older woman scurried behind us like a frantic rat on tracks seconds before a train arrives. She knocked on the door of the house and was let in instantly. This was it for me.

"Can I wait out here?" I asked.

"Of course you're going to wait out here, they don't know you."

"Well I mean I kinda look like a little girl so I highly doubt they'd be intimidated but anyways...here's $20 get two bags for me and two for yourself," I said while fishing the $20 bill out of my jacket pocket. Not tipping him for his services in this mundane realm would've been rude.

Less than two minutes later he reappeared outside. He handed over my two heroin bags. A skull and crossbones stamp marked the tiny, white paper bags. Darkness eclipsed my intuition as he placed the heroin bags in my sweaty palm. I'd been toying around in dark matters for years but that binding moment struck me more profoundly than any before. My sinking gut conveyed some tragic news to me, that this was the beginning of the end. Nonetheless, grazing my fingers over the paper heroin bags made my surface-level emotion of sheer relief (the emotion I'd been craving) impossible to deny. Falling asleep in a benevolent fashion sounded so enchanting I wasn't even startled by the prospect of not waking up. The two of us headed back towards the late hour's Chinese food shop.

"So what were you doing out here?" he asked.

"Working," I said. Further elaboration was unnecessary given our whereabouts.

"In that case, I could give you these two and a place to get high."

"Oh I'm done for the night actually, I have a place to get back to."

"Do you have a phone number?"

"No, I don't have a phone. I'm too poor for one right now," I answered. That was a lie. I *did* own a phone. Admitting to owning a valuable item such as a phone may have compelled him to put a gun to the side of my head as a way of asking me to charitably donate my belongings to him.

If you were to ask me what it means to be street smart I'd tell you it's all about knowing who to trust and knowing not to trust them any longer than necessary—and never show all your cards. We reached the entrance of the El Train station. He told me to get home safely as if that was still in my cards for the night; as if I wasn't as good as dead already.

restless, restless, restless arms
do not be alarmed
tundra heart
melt

OLIVIA J. KIERS
SWEET DREAM

I dreamt I dropped
a yellow, 4-lb. bag
of Domino Sugar,
and it burst, millions
of granulated, white-hot
stars whirling past their big bang.

The universe expands, a sweet
accident across linoleum,
and I cannot contain it.
Arch, whorl, loop—
galactic fingerprints
make it worse, leave sticky traces,
cause buckles and voids,
heap nebulas, scramble
surfaces like an empty
paper bag crumpling
in on itself.

ELINOR CLARK
CLOUD WATCHING

Catch the deluge
in the veined blue
of the sky
cumli cumuli,
large and fluffy.
Huggable they say,
eyes sliding
down her body.
She rests the bags,
plastic bottoms
leaking onto frost-studded
dirt. Splays stiffened hands,
twinkle, twinkle, shake away
the ache of winter's needle chill.
Winds like ivy over hips
but she doesn't rush,
watching shadows paint
a shaky V, arrows guiding
from above.

SOPHIE HOSS
VAN GOGH'S STARRY NIGHT OVER THE RHONE

I've got an imagination like you wouldn't believe, my grandfather confided.
When I look up at the sky, I pretend each star is a cottage
on the edge of a black river.
His hand was bony and birdlike when it squeezed mine.
I think this painting may be an illusion—
maybe each of those oily yellow stars glinting on the water
is just another house on another river.
Maybe it's my grandfather's soul, still in this world,
borne around the bend by that soft current
one star at a time.

JAMES B. NICOLA
SWIMMERS IN MAINE

I'll never meet them again
    or know their names
as I don't live in Maine
    and if I do go back

to swim it will surely be
    to some other beach
and not before sunrise, when I arrived one day
    hours early—

I had woken
    long before the alarm,
and wanted to get going anyway—
    and decided

to jump in the ocean to kill
    an hour. And was surprised
to find that I was not alone.
    I don't mean fish

but from the sea at Wells there popped
    up one by one like so many tadpoles
youths glistening in bodysuits of jet
    body surfing

in the chill
    of the early
twilight.
    How they teased

me, with my flesh exposed, but then said they
    were surprised that I lasted a whole mile
in the icy brine. But I did. I asked them
    if they did this every morning. They said Yeah,

all summer. I told them that if I
    were going to make it a daily thing,
I'd probably invest in one of those rubber suits,
    too, to make them feel a littler better

and not so much like the wusses
    I knew they weren't. O the way we had turned
Not in an instant like a school of guppies
    But like morning glories, or corn in hot oil,

back after back, supine in the Atlantic
     head to shore each one—still, not surfing
now—while the sun popped up
     its burnished head with a primal-screamy silence
and for ten minutes—five—fifteen—
     we lay parallel and were as One—
yes, I among them! even if it might
     have seemed to the sluggish, condescending sky

that I and my
     pinkness were of
an entirely other
     race.

BATHROOM MIRROR

These creases next to the eyes—
a palm to read to know how this will end:
fairy dust and melatonin, beauty fading
like a polaroid of high school
prom, teeth still vivid like those
on a skull. In case of emergency,
frame the photo and place it
on your casket so everyone can see
how this was only inevitable.

You filled your head with songs and sugar,
licked the limericks of time until
a hole appeared in your tongue,
and the gravity of the meaning
washes over you and wets your hair
so you slick it back and parade past
the mirror and imagine a grandstand,
handkerchiefs waving down packed
avenues, funeral dirges disrupting
the birds near a man sitting alone
on a bench, eating chips in the park,
feeding pigeons from the bag.

FRED JOHNSON
A PASSING CAR

Two strings of light
above the carriageway:
white   violet
blue.

Waiting—not for dawn
or for pastel spring,
but for the hoarse call
of daily prayer.

It has been a year now,
and the starlings still
have not returned.

In their place: cafes,
empty lots, the factory
a leviathan risen,
damp with terrible age.

Sometimes,
the sirens go on all night.

It was England, after all,
or Ohio, or it doesn't
matter where—

only that the view
had moved on, arm round
a woman you knew, once,

leaving the window
empty and you
beyond the frame, staring.

In the lonely backyard
of winter, the tire swing
hangs silent and still,
tired of trying to strike up
conversations with snowdrifts
who never respond anyway,
and pretty much immune now
to the neighborhood squirrels,
who just walk all over her
like she wasn't even there.
With nothing else to do then,
she dozes off, swaying in and out
of vivid, full-color dreams
where she sails rider after rider
through a bright kaleidoscope
of untethered delight,
the sun warm on her sidewalls
and the breeze in her treads
as she glides by and by into waking,
and then just to find herself
shivering and shrouded
by a heap of new-fallen snow.

DOROTHY NEAGLE
IF MY MOTHER WERE ONE THING

potatoes under straw
in black earth
watermelon on the porch
cans of Canada Dry
sunglasses – red
shaped like hearts
horsefly, dragonfly, mosquito
milk-soaked cereal
bee stings, baking soda
Calamine lotion
aloe plant split open
stone walls, weeds
snapdragons just planted
iris, peony
a pyramid of strawberries
no shoes, or
shoes that slip-on only
summer sound of bugs
a distant tractor
all of it stuck
under the heat
pulsing, haying time
baling twine
fans drown out
everything inside
panting dogs
cats in the low,
cool dust of the barn
freckles up and down her arms
root-beer-colored
nicotine stain
on the middle finger
of her right hand
left hand empty because
she never wore
a wedding ring

2001

I feel like I buried Dad twice. The first time was when I brought him to a nursing home.

"Now *you* should take care of your mother," Dad said while I drove.

"Why don't you answer me?" He asked after a pause.

I was choked with tears; I could not even hug him. I just took his hand in mine and kept steering the wheel with the other hand until the next turn.

*   *   *

Dad had a quadruple bypass two years ago. Then he got stomach cancer, and it was surgically removed. Dad got stronger and even started walking outside. We felt relieved. Then he lost his appetite. At first, it seemed like a whim: Dad always liked to eat. Mom cooked anything he asked for, and yet he ate less and less. Then he agreed only to liquid food. Then he refused to eat at all. Doctors shrugged.

Mom and I screamed at him, hoping he would pick up his will to overcome the disease. Mom was desperate; she fed him like a baby: "Take another spoon, yet another spoon; do it for me!" Sometimes my daughter managed to convince him to eat a little. She was the last one who could make him smile.

Dad got weaker and weaker; he slept almost all the time. At some point, he could not stand up anymore. I would go to my parents at night to bring Dad to the bathroom before putting him to bed. He hid his face in my chest when I lifted him from the toilet. Once he kissed my hand. I did not scream at him after that. When he developed incontinence, Mom could not take care of him anymore; she was eighty at the time.

*   *   *

Dad spent five weeks in the nursing home before he died. Mom said she wanted to lie beside him one day, and I bought two plots in a Jewish cemetery. On the funeral day, a few of our relatives and my parents' neighbors gathered in a funeral home. The rabbi said some nice things about Dad that I had told him a day earlier. Then we drove to the cemetery.

The rabbi said a short prayer. Then the cemetery workers put the casket into the grave.

"Papa, that's all?" my sobbing daughter asked.

I hugged her and stone-faced Mom. We went home.

My son was born a few months later. From behind, his onion-shaped head looked exactly like Dad's. I have few regrets in my life. One of them is that Dad died before he could see his grandson.

*   *   *

2017

My Mom turns ninety-five soon.

"I don't believe I'm so old," she tells me. "I think I'm ninety-two."

She is not ninety-two anymore. Three years ago, she was informing me about what was happening in the world every time I called her. Then she lost interest in anything but classical music; then she stopped listening to music; she just spent days in a recliner consumed by her thoughts. One day I found that Mom could not get up off the recliner anymore. Then I brought her to the same nursing home where Dad died.

Mom's memory has shrunk into several disconnected islands. My family inhabits one of them.

"How is your daughter? How is your son?" She always asks when I visit her.

"How is your wife? She never visits me. What's her name?" At least she remembers that I'm married.

"How is your family life?" She continues to inquire.

"Everything is fine." I haven't told her that we had separated; she would be very upset.

"Good," she says, "it's important to have a strong family."

"Marina sends you her regards," I tell her.

"Who is Marina?" Mom asks.

"She is your niece, your brother's daughter."

"I don't remember," she says sadly. "Where does she live?"

"In Moscow."

"I remember Moscow," Mom smiles. "I was young; I had a boyfriend in high school; I started early." She giggles; then glances at me. "It's not what you think. We were just walking hand in hand and kissing good night."

I wonder why she still remembers her high school sweetheart but not her niece.

"Well, he later broke up with me," she sighs. "He wanted to pursue a diplomatic career, but I was, you know, the daughter of an enemy of the people."

Well, we never forget betrayal. I kiss Mom on the forehead.

*   *   *

Mom was born in Germany and came to the USSR in her early teens. My grandpa was smart enough to flee with his family from Germany soon after the Nazis came to power. He had chosen the wrong direction… My grandparents at first were treated as political refugees. But soon grandpa was arrested and convicted of "suspicion in espionage for Germany." Grandpa did not survive Gulag. He was not even fifty when he died.

All Soviet high school students were expected to become members of the communist youth organization. At pompous meetings, children of "enemies of the people" had to publicly denounce their parents.

"I won't do this. My father is an honest, innocent man," Mom said to the school youth leader.

"Don't come to school on the day of the meeting," he advised.

Decent people helped my family survive political terror and even preserve some dignity. Yet living in fear during her teenage years forever influenced Mom. She was always suspicious of postmen, superintendents, curious neighbors, or anyone who might turn out to be a snitch.

My uncle, Mom's brother, had become a youth boxing champion while growing up on tough Moscow streets. "I've got great practice while fighting everyone who mocked my German accent," he grinned.

He was mobilized to the Red Army right after the school prom. Germans invaded a month later. After some training, my uncle, with a group of paratroopers disguised in German uniform, sneaked across the front line. They were blowing up trains, railroads, bridges - anything that helped Nazis to move forward.

"First, we had to take out the guards. It was my job. I spoke native German and could approach them without causing suspicions. And we had to be quiet, so we mostly used bayonets," my uncle recalled his bloody war experience.

By the war's end, my uncle achieved the rank of captain. After returning to Moscow, he put on his uniform with all his medals and went to the Chief Prosecutor's office. Soon Grandpa was posthumously exonerated.

*   *   *

"Your father was a good man," Mom returns to the recent past. "We had such a beautiful life."

"She does not remember anything," I sigh.

Dad was born in Latvia. He managed to flee to Russia when Nazis invaded but all Jews in the small town where his parents used to live were killed. Germans didn't have to bother with executions; there were volunteers among the neighbors. They received houses and other belongings from their victims.

At the end of the war, Dad served in engineering troops. He met Mom in Moscow while repairing the building damaged by bombing where she used to live. They married and moved to Riga after Dad was demobilized.

Dad was devoted to the family. He did the shopping, washed dishes, and helped Mom choose new clothes. But he was paranoid about KGB for the last twenty years of his life. Not only did *they* watch him, but *they* also reminded him of this at every opportunity. If, for example, my parents talked about a neighbor and then Dad saw that neighbor on the street, this was a sign that KGB listened to the parents' conversation and ordered the neighbor to confront Dad. Nothing changed when my parents moved to the USA. *They* were everywhere. We asked him to go to the doctor. He refused. *They* controlled doctors, too. Mom carried that burden until his death; she could not imagine living without him.

*   *   *

"Why did you come without a jacket?" Mom asks.

"It's spring, mama; it's warm outside," I tell her.

"Is it spring already?" She exclaims.

I kiss her again.

"Don't get upset when I'm gone," Mom returns me the kiss. "It's not life anymore."

*   *   *

She will die two weeks later.

MICHAELA MAYER
FAMILY DYSFUNCTION PANTOUM
In memory of Grace Matheny Mayer

On a glorious sundown day in March I learned
my grandmother was dying. That bitter fruit
who made my father, cruel-toothed tormentor
of my mother and sister and me, would go.

My grandmother was dying. That bitter fruit
squeezed down to pulp by seizures, now blind
to my mother and sister and me, would go,
and I had not called since summertime.

Squeezed down to pulp by seizures, now blind,
my dying grandmother lay in hospice alone,
and I had not called since summertime.
I sat hollowed on the grass and could not cry.

My dying grandmother lay in hospice alone,
she who deflected jabs at my fattened figure.
I sat hollowed on the grass and could not cry.
Kind was not the word for her, and yet—

she'd deflected jabs at my fattened figure.
One summer my parents paid me to mind her.
Kind was not the word for Grandmother, and yet—
she'd softened then: withering to withered.

In the green grass, in the gentle breeze
on a glorious sundown day in March I learned
of her looming demise and could not cry. Going,
who made my father, our cruel-toothed tormentor:
I mind.

TUESDAY TAYLOR
THEY SAY I DON'T KNOW NOTHING
Urban Appalachian Girl

about
unity
    or
white trash
    or immigrants
        or children of freed slaves,
who fought-
    together,
or how our own government
d
 r
  o
   p
   p
    e
   d,
   BOMBS
        on Americans.

Nope, know nothing about
survival,
    or
squirrel gravy
    or
Appalachian Drag Queens
    or
beauty
    or
white classism
        & white privilege
    or
meth-making,
    or
pretty teeth
    or
2019 4-wheel jacked-up trucks parked in front of rundown trailers
        & pride
    or
belief
    or
hillbilly hustlers with gold fronts
    or
cooper hunting

or
food stamps being sold
        or
ginseng digging
        or
drug traffickers looking like teachers and sounding like radio hosts.

I don't know a damn thing,
about coal mining.
or 10,000 marching men,
or 10,000 men battled the police-
& coal companies-
for 10 days,
or a million shots fired,
or America's 2nd largest armed civic uprise-
since the Civil War, happened in some hick town-
in West Virginia.

Only Black Lung I know of,
comes from smoking too many rolled-up cigarettes.
Jasper is my grandfather's name, he's a prejudiced liberal,
corrected his accent, didn't want folks saying,
he don't know nary
                        about Appalachia.

Blair Mountain,
wasn't she some toothless harlot,
got her cherry popped on the side of some mountain?
When she was young, she looked identical to
Jennifer Gardner.
Heard she sold her children for a
facelift, but Blair don't
know nothing about
sacrifice
        or
prayer
        or
poverty pimping
        or
resiliency
        or
dandelion tea
        or
moonshine
        or
deer season
        or
3 eyed fish
        or

granny's being mommas

                & sister-cousins

or

brown beans, fried taters and cornbread

    or

flatfooting

    or

Chuck Yeager

    or

Spanky Roberts

    or

brown babies with blue eyes

    or

child incarceration

    or

opioid addicts

    or

Ain't No Sunshine When She's Gone,

    or

pimps killing whores on West Washington street

    or

       singing murder ballads

              after Sunday School.

One day I was told:
You got to be smart at something,
who am I fooling,
I grew up in the projects,
I don't know a
Damn Thing.

RC deWINTER
INFECTION

i cut my finger
hauling out the trash
there were four heavy bags to go
and i could smell rain

i have no idea which bag
was my assassin
two of them broke on the way
up the hill

by the time i realized
i was bleeding
i was a circus tent
striped in red

now there is a furrow
on the fourth finger of my right hand
a death's-head skull grinning at me
spitting out a devil's fountain of blood

and in that wound no doubt
lie septic microorganisms
hitching a ride through my bloodstream
despite my copious washing

ah well when the soul is as sick as mine
what matters the sickness of the body
let them be conjoined
melded in a twinship of pathology

STEWART LINDSTROM
POLYETHYLENE REFLECTS ON ITS ORIGINS, THE POST-WAR
AMERICAN ECONOMY, AND HUMANKIND'S FINAL DESTINY

You can't imagine what it's like to wake
to the news that you are malleable, that you
will become both baking implements

and death-tool. That after the high priests
have weaved your flesh into the fabric
of the new reality, after you are so ubiquitous

as to be the stuff of soft drink containers
and Bakelite, after you've been smeared
across car frames and made up the plane cockpits

aimed at East Asia, you will not be allowed
to die. Who did I kill that I should be cursed
to wander? I was the perfect patriot, wasn't I?

I exemplified Kennedy's inaugural maxim: I asked
nothing of the country and gave myself wholly
to every cause. And yet, where are my medals,

my honors, my pensions? I was the chrysalis
within which this America
was born. Something so new that you

did not know what to do with me.
After the war smoke faded, you gave me over
to computer parts and pre-packaged food.

You partook of me manically.
You stocked up on my body, collecting
my flesh with a zealot's fervor.

Soon I was everywhere. And yet,
even after all I did for you, you made me a refugee.
You tossed my body into the seabeds. I was bitter

that I should be so neglected. Sea creatures ingested
my body, taking part in the post-war communion
unbeknownst to themselves.

But here is my revenge:
Now you too take part in the eucharist, secondhand. Soon
your stomachs will be so lined

with my flesh that you too will not rot.
You will lie in the seabeds, gorged
on the immortal consequences of your excess.

You will look at your cold hands in horror, knowing
you live in the last human century.
The Plast-ocene fast approaching, the age

of he who remade you: Cain. I will boast, I will jeer,
I will shout from the housetops: "Welcome
to the eon devoid of death or life,

to the desert of empty gestures at men and women
who once were made of flesh. Who became slaves
to their last creation. Who woke

out of the hazy factory of centuries to lifeless skies.
Who, weeping, realized, at long last,
that a demon was hatching from the gray waves before them.

And the demon was a man.
And the demon had forty mouths.
And each mouth hung open and insatiable."

ALOLIKA A. DUTTA
A WRITTEN TRANSCRIPT OF SEVEN PICTURES FROM DELHI

20th June 2019
New Delhi, India

mulberry silk draped over dreary dirty skin   arms covered in green glass
bangles   estranged women with scalps soaked in *sindoor*
like the tongue of *kali*
          the land beneath *jallianwala bagh* on april 13th 1919
          the lanes of *bengal* on the last day of *durga's* residence
     and the reddened foreheads of devotees who line the streets of a city clothed in *mughal*
architecture islamic chants and a distant mourning-
                         a simmering refrain heard in the hallways of a mausoleum   the
conversations between the door and the widow and the tourists and the travellers who eavesdrop on
a grief four hundred years old-

the synchronised *azaan* echoing from lane to lane from bazaar to bazaar from within mosques and
cathedrals built beside universities-
          wombs of homegrown heresy-
rectangular pieces of cloth held by hands covered in wandering marks of blue ink   women in *khaki*
standing across from those in *saffron* in white in red
               the young standing across from the old in shirts printed with   the face of
che-

on an adjacent street- a group of young wives dressed in floral-printed synthetic *sarees* of magenta and
watermelon pink   a *ghoonghat* pulled over the head and a red *bindi* between the eyebrows like the
moon amid a lunar eclipse-

a northeastern woman vending colouring books under a banyan tree   her skin beads with
sweat   a collection of scars and stretch marks across her breasts: maps   parched land   sheets
of aged paper   dried drops of blood on white bed sheets occupied by tired bodies in decayed
marriages   agony dances on her forehead as she sits there breasts bared   a six
month old clings to her body   sucking at her flesh   skin against skin   dusky like a
desert in the afternoon   the winds of *kalbaishakhi*   the soil in assam   the faces of the
indigenous   she calls out to the strangers on the street with a hand resting on a knee another
holding her child an indifferent kind of liberty-

walls stained with tobacco covered in scattered campaign posters   half-ripped   an abandoned
child staring at a series of peculiar shapes assembled in straight lines read into loudspeakers and
microphones at evening demonstrations
          by men in half-sleeved cotton kurtas and beige vests   by women in imported
cotton sarees   by unknown people who address the poor from a pedestal and speak of liberation
in a colonial language-

at a distance   a barber's shop with brick walls painted in shades of blue sky falling over a town and a child staring at the repeated hand movements of his father between conversations in broken *khariboli   bangla*   and   *urdu*   a set of framed pictures above a mirror covered in fingerprints   imperial reminders of 90,000 deaths   a yellowed photograph of a palace built for the viceroy- a monument of sandstone that still houses fear within the five hundred seventy-three square miles of land that still carry the regret of 1857 that still home the poetry of *ghalib* and *dagh* that will always wear the scent of a religion abandoned-

the minarets the tombs the roads the corridors the bicycle rickshaws the scorned hawkers and
        the sight of a young girl in a *burqa* and *niqab* within a taxi with yellow paisley printed seats-
            the quiet lifting of the *niqab*   red lipstick unbottled and briskly shifted underneath *kohl*-lined eyes that move to the rhythm of her hands until the niqab is repositioned the bottle returned to a hidden compartment of a glossy black handbag and hands folded in anticipation- a silent kind of defiance.

this is delhi-   the deep plangent sound of an empty earthen vessel being filled with well water   the hollow screeching of the wind making way through the peeling edge of a locked wooden door   stealthy footsteps on a muddy field   unclasping of a sweat-soaked cotton blouse temple bells ringing at midnight-   the beginning to a riot

delhi-

the sound of *dissent*

simmering.

DAVID SWERDLOW
FORMS OF TERROR

1.

Birds don't gawk when I force
an opossum from our patio with a shot
from the garden hose. It's tough
for him to leave the dark circle

where fat has leaked from our grill
onto the brick. His pink pointed nose
and black marble eyes give no
understanding of trespass, though

he backs away like someone who
believes he had been misunderstood
then scuttles uphill through
our rock garden, the perennial

flowers twisting around his form
until he's gone—me with the hose.

2.

My daughter couldn't bear the young man
whose eyes never focused, who smiled
at me in the parking lot of the New Baptist
Church where I vote, asking me
if I'd write-in his name for the auditor,
his head tilted, November's cold
in his hand that I chose not to shake
because he'd terrorized this person I love.

A week after he was elected,
just past the red-tailed hawk's familiar
perch by the highway, blood soaked
the median where the white-haired woman
died. The young man, stoned
and drunk, crashed his car into hers
early that afternoon—vehicular
homicide, yellow buses not far
away, not yet filling with children,
her husband alone in the sun.

3.

Doubtful the blackbirds
over the schoolyard wonder
who has a shotgun in his truck
and plans to take down the sky.

ANDREW HANSON
ARS POETICA

Pithy anxiety, the tingle
of bullet shards
sprinkled on ice-cream,
board game banter
after the power has gone out.
The snail's trail
as it shines thinner than the
skim on a beach. A child,
skittering out
in a forest
familiar as the veins
on the back of her hand.
They don't talk
about the hangman's metaphysics;
Yet, poets cock a top hat, twist
a cigar, and tease out
the twisted bones
of love and the hard cup
of jazz in a saxophone,
the cyan shine of pennies,
chucked in a well
deeper than ambition....

Kee Chamisa's cup of coffee was halfway to his lips when he noticed an odd stir among other Navajo people gathered in the cafe. The ripple washed over those at a table near the corner booth where he ate breakfast with former Council members from western Dinétah. Stanley Tsosie edged his chair closer, as Kee and his companions waited expectantly. "Darlene Yazzie had a dream and got people shook up."

Bidzii Haskie asked the nature of the dream. Stanley excused himself and made his way across the restaurant. He returned. "Mrs. Roanhorse heard it from her neighbor who looks in on Mrs. Yazzie. She wasn't the only one who had the dream." Kee and Bidzii exchanged startled glances.

"Mrs. Yazzie's friend, Pauletta K., a Hopi woman had a dream, too," Stanley said. His eyebrows reared like dark stallions. "Scene by scene identical."

Kee leaned across the table and nearly drug his cedar bead necklace through his bowl of squash soup. Stanley said, "The dreams were about going out to say morning prayers and lots of stuff was missing."

"What did the thieves take?" Harrison Charlie asked.

"Vehicles, for one thing." The one-time legislators agreed they weren't surprised. Bidzii said he was surprised the ladies were still driving.

Stanley cooled a sip of coffee while shaking his head from side to side. "*All* the vehicles were gone. Not a chidí in sight!" He thoughtfully tapped the rim of his ceramic coffee mug. "Other stuff was gone, too, like satellite dishes off rooftops."

Harrison couldn't help politely interjecting an observation. "Sounds like Kit Carson 2.0."

Stanley's eyes glittered over a gleeful smile. "Well, it might seem like another bilagáana Big Take, but it gets better." He forked into a sling of hash browns and chewed reflectively.

"Okay, Stan, we're not voting on this. Just please tell us," Kee said in a tone meant to show patience he did not feel. Stanley signaled a bit more delay with an upraised index finger as he speared a bite of mutton.

Harrison groaned and started to get up. "I'm going over to ask Mrs. Roanhorse directly."

"Okay, gentlemen, here it is," Stanley said in a deep, dramatic voice. "What there *was* in these dreams was buffalo."

"A buffalo?" Bidzii quizzed.

"Lots and *lots* of buffalo. Everywhere the ladies looked, clear to the horizon, buffalo were grazing in the grass. Thick, tall grass!" Kee was excited.

"I like the sound of that!" Stanley nodded.

"Deer and antelope, too, like that bilagáana song. And the water was running deep in Dinnebito Wash."

Harrison got a faraway gleam in his eyes. "Sounds like Dinétah paradise."

Stanley agreed. "Maybe this is the Diné version of the Ghost Dance vision except the bilagáana are still here but they don't have vehicles, either."

The others smiled as the conversation ran to speculation of how the dream message might stir people to action and how far it would travel.

Kee was set to fly back to California but he needed to do something before he left Dinétah. He called ahead and arranged to visit the two buffalo dreamers. They were at Darlene Yazzie's hogan just over the boundary on the Diné side of 'Jeddito Island,' a small area of mostly Navajo people allowed to remain inside the Hopi apportionment when the land was partitioned in the 1974 Lands Settlement Act. As if it settled *any*thing, Kee mused. He wanted to hear from their lips what they thought the dream had to say.

Kee parked along the dirt road and walked through patches of greasewood gilded by deep buttery blooms. A breeze stirred Grama grass and rippled the dark green canopies of junipers growing sporadically among the low hills.

"Yá'át'ééh abiní," he called out from a few dozen yards before he got to the door. Darlene appeared and ushered him inside the hogan. Her home was only a few hundred feet from Mrs. K's house, who was there with Darlene. She set a kettle of water on the small wood stove at the center of the hogan.

Moments later, tea was poured into three non-matching ceramic mugs. The women glanced at each other and Mrs. Yazzie told Kee the dream was a call to native people to return to the ancestors' ways. Not horses and wagons, though that might be interesting, she chuckled. She noted rodeos were a big deal so maybe horses did have a role to play. Mrs. K. warmed her fingers around the mug and said Hopis still have the Buffalo Dance as one of their Kachina ceremonies and sometimes it's used to heal sick people.

Kee asked if the dream meant giving up modern gizmos like satellite TV and vehicles. Both women shrugged and after a time Mrs. Yazzie said, "Maybe that's gotta happen for some people to live traditionally."

Mrs. K. said it was good to think healthy substitutes for a lot of what people buy from stores. She thought of something else. "We don't need clocks or calendars in our houses because we've got 'em out there." She gestured with her head toward the window, which framed a bright, turquoise sky.

The women said when they were actively teaching, they'd take children outdoors and help them figure out the season and time of day by looking where the sun was and what the plants were doing in their growth cycle. They reminded the youngsters if they paid attention to what Earth is doing they'd know the when and what of life. Mrs. Yazzie had another thought. Maybe the buffalo dream encouraged people to look to their relations with each other and with local Earth. "We can be more reliant on ourselves and each other." That was pretty much it and Kee thanked the ladies for their wisdom and also for the tea.

*　　　*　　　*

Kee flew back to the regional tribal information office in Northern California, where he worked and prepared to share his exciting news. His colleague, Emma, blurted, "You'll never guess what's happening!" Kee considered the improbable. "Some kind of dream people are having about an Indian paradise?"

The woman registered astonishment. "How did you—was it going around Dinétah, too?" Kee confirmed it was. He made his rounds of several tiny reserves in the region and in each place found buffalo dreams occurring there, too.

He consulted the board members of his employer, the Redwood Coast Indigenous Peoples Council, who agreed to share the story with other native people who read his column in a national Native American newspaper. He spent several days and half of two nights trying to get it right. He wanted to be accurate and not overstate the significance of the message. He wrote in part:

"Many indigenous people pay close attention to their dreams. Often, if a dream is significant in some way it will be shared with family and close friends and maybe a medicine person. For generations, dreams have been sources of important information and have sometimes suggested options for future actions.

A woman on the Navajo Nation had a dream a few weeks ago. Later that day she told it to a good friend who is a neighbor and a member of the Hopi tribe. The other woman was surprised and shared her dream, which was almost identical in its essential features. Within days there were reports of other dreamers in various regions, including people from other tribes such as Paiute, Havasupai, Camp Verde Apache, Tohono O'Odham, Lakota, and Northwestern Shoshone. At first, it was thought the dreams were confined to people in the western part of the continent, but then word arrived that members of tribes in the Northeast, including Chippewa, Onondaga, and Passamaquoddy, reported similar dreams.

Here is how the two elders, Mrs. Darlene Yazzie (Diné) and Mrs. Pauletta K. (Hopi) shared their dreams with this reporter:

'In the dream, I woke up and went outside to say my morning prayers like I always do. Everything looked pretty normal but there were some empty spots.

Pauletta K added, "I couldn't see any cars or trucks parked around or hear any moving along the highway."

Mrs. Yazzie confirmed that. "That's right—no chidis." Both women said the satellite dishes were also missing from the rooftops. They said something *was* there that usually was not—buffalo, lots of buffalo.

Mrs. K. found this as a surprise because her great-grandmother told her the buffalo have been gone from Hopitutskwa for 150 years.

Mrs. Yazzie said she heard similar things from her Aunt. Because the reappearance of the bison is considered one of the most significant parts of the dreams, people who report these nightly events are being called the Buffalo Dreamers.

When asked what they thought about the dreams, Mrs. K. said she was happy in her dream to see buffalo and deer and antelope in abundance in Hopiland, and there was also a sweet sound she doesn't hear as much these days. "It was a kind of rhythmic hiss with a deeper voice. I looked around some more and saw women tossing kernels of blue corn from hand-woven baskets to let chaff fly away in the process of making piki bread. Women still do that in our tribe of course but it was good to see many more younger girls learning how to make piki in the old way." She said the dream was like an invitation for people to consider what is most important and what they need to live for and what they need less of.

Mrs. Yazzie shared similar feelings and said if people spent less time driving around or watching TV shows there would be more time for social gatherings and paying attention to what the land needs to be healthy.

Written representations of other buffalo dreams showed very similar ideas about the significance of those dreams throughout indigenous communities. One person who wished to remain anonymous suggested this could be the modern-day version of the Ghost Dance.

One thing is for sure: excitement is awakening native people across the country to new possibilities.

* * *

Kee was surprised how many times the story ran in various native newspapers and magazines and was heard on native radio stations. One of the editors in an editorial seriously considered whether this might be a genuine equivalent of the 1890s Ghost Dance. And that speculation caught the interest of mainstream media. Suddenly, Kee's office received dozens of media requests for comment on whether some kind of Indian rebellion was brewing. He deferred most questions to Board members on the Council, but some background context he supplied in the news release was picked up by wire services and one quote, in particular, seemed to spark public attention: "This is not like Wovoka's vision in the 1890s where the world gets rolled up like a carpet with the white people in it." In typical media style, headlines turned the statement inside out and refashioned it as a statement. Too often, and to Kee's dismay, it appeared as a headline. "Does Buffalo Dreamer Movement Mean White Race to Disappear?"
Kee sent out another news release with permission of the Board in which he clarified his statement. It felt odd, quoting himself, but he did

not want to misrepresent what he felt was a profound and beneficial truth about the Buffalo Dreamers. "Native people," he wrote, "who have had this dream describe it as a call for unity and positive action among indigenous people. There is nothing in it to suggest any ill will towards non-Indians."

Despite all, the controversy grew and finally, the Board asked Kee to call a press conference to straighten things out. The meeting room in the back of the NCIPC building was full at the appointed time and reporters and others filled all of the folding chairs. Some even stood along the rear wall. There were bright lights from the TV cameras and a few reporters from the international press. Kee felt nervous and apologized to the Board for attracting such attention but most of them were pleased with the mainstream media turning out like this to respond to a native matter. Sekia Pinola, a friend and a member of a southern Pomo tribal group up the coast, sat next to Kee and tried to help ease his anxiety. She told him there were some activists from the Lakota Nation in the room, which somehow only made Kee feel even more nervous.

Many questions were directed to an elder member of the Agua Caliente Cahuilla tribe, who lived near Palm Springs. She reported the dream and said it was real close to the one described by "the ladies in Arizona." She stood up and faced the reporters and said her hope was "Indian people remember who they are down deep."

A reporter wanted to know if she felt non-Indians would be affected by the message and the elder grinned and said it would be a good thing if everyone did more walking and less driving because there wouldn't be as many people suffering from the disease. "Red, Yellow, Green, or White—suffering is suffering and the less of it the better," she said, sitting down.

A tall figure emerged from the shadows in the backroom and, with a deep voice tinged in tension, directed his question to Kee. He said he was from Lakota country over at White River. His hair was long and shiny as obsidian and Kee could see tattoos up and down his arms. "Why in your news release does it sound like Indian people are supposed to get rid of the few things they have?"

Kee stood and saw several of the cameras swing his way. "Well, sir, I appreciate the question but what I put in there was my best effort to accurately relay what the ladies said who I first met in Dinetah. I tried to be careful not to add my thoughts about the message of the dream."

The young man shook his head, pursed his lips, and made a sound that to Kee was like a growl. "Maybe you weren't careful enough." He let the accusation stand.

There were murmurs in the crowd. Kee felt his chest tighten. He cleared his throat and asked, "What do you think the press release should say?"

The Lakota man laughed sardonically. "I don't think there ought to be *any* press release. These dreams are *wakan* and they shouldn't be treated this way."

Kee asked, "Do you know people from your region who had this dream?"

The man shrugged. "Maybe, maybe not."

"We released this news to native media because it feels important. People can make of it what they will," Kee said, summoning confidence into his tone.

The tall man shook his head slowly. "There was a message in the dreams and you played it down." The tone was accusing. Kee blushed, felt Sekia's hand slide around his forearm, and squeeze—a subtle reassurance. Kee cleared his throat. "You mean the mention of the Ghost Dance?"

The Lakota man allowed a tight smile.

Kee spoke rapidly before his confidence flagged. "That was a comment heard here one day by a tribal member from a Rancheria. It was just a comment. It's in the release because it is on some people's minds."

The Lakota man laughed. His face seemed lit from within. He spoke in an open sneer. "It's on a *lot* of people's minds. There's honest power in the vision of the world getting rolled up and all the wasicun's toxic stuff with it." He paused, then dramatically added, "and wasicuns, too."

Now the crowd erupted in murmurs and several reporters shouted questions to the Lakota man. Kee tried to regain his moderator's role. "Excuse me, please. Please, can we have one question at a time?"

The Lakota activist raised his voice and directed it at Kee. "My question for you is why you're acting like such an apple?"

"You do not know me. If you did, you'd see I do my best to convey the will of native people in this region through the channels we have available to us. I'm no apple," Key replied. And then he was surprised to hear himself say, "I'm hosh bineest'ą' prickly pear cactus fruit—red on the inside and the outside."

The Lakota man was not having it. "If you really believed that you'd be doing more than writing little press releases, P.R. guy. Indian people have been sending messages to Washington or other wasicun encampments for centuries and all we get is more broken promises. When you try to wrap the strong spirit of the Buffalo Dream in your news release you are binding its real force. For that, I turn my back on you." He pivoted, raised an arm with a clenched fist, and pumped it four times. He began to move through the crowd toward the back door. A female reporter wriggled through the assembly and planted herself in front of him, holding a microphone under his chin. "Samantha Forsyth, Channel Seven News. Do you believe the only way forward for native people is away from white culture?"

The Lakota man tapped his chest. "Do I believe? When the buffalo return, when the Buffalo People return, the Indian people can shake off their shackles and rise above."

The reporter's brow furrowed. Then she asked, "And what are those of us who come from European culture supposed to do?"

"Get back on the boat." He brushed past her and made for the door, as the murmurs grew louder.

Kee turned to the Board members as they huddled in anxious conversation about what to do next. Kee apologized. A few reporters were closing in on them and Kee was desperate to get some guidance from his elders on the Board.

One of the members was a founder and said the Council could lose nonprofit status if they became known as a political organization. "This sounded like politics, young man." He shook his head solemnly and two of the other Board members agreed that the way Kee framed things did sound like the Council was taking a strong political position. Another elder reminded Kee there were two sizeable grants in the loop now and all this implied hostility to Anglos could harm their chances of securing the much-needed funding.

Kee's mind churned. He didn't want to be at the center of a controversy that was not of his making, even if others thought his handling had fanned flames of racial tension. Maybe the right thing to do was resign. Take himself out of the picture so things could quiet down. A voice from somewhere inside asked whether things quieting down would be a good or unfortunate turn of events. He writhed in indecision and fear and was ready to excuse himself and disappear at least for a while. Sekia tapped his shoulder and lifted a chin in the direction of the back of the room.

There was a commotion there and Kee could see the back of the Lakota activist's head, his long hair swishing side to side as he approached the doorway. He stopped. Or was halted. There were low voices, female, Kee decided. The Lakota man's head angled down, both arms rose in a gesture that could have signaled either frustration or confusion. He slowly turned around. Just above the crowd, Kee could see the tops of two heads flanking the tall Lakota man. He was being escorted to the front of the room.

Now the assembly fell silent and at last, the crowd parted. Kee gasped. Grasping the forearm of the Lakota activist were Mrs. Yazzie and Mrs. K. He called out, "My Grandmothers, how? Why? We are so honored to have you here." Darlene gave a small wave and said they had come on the dog bus. First time ever.

Mrs. K laughed. "The big Greyhound bus has a bathroom in it. Really nice."

They promised to provide more background on how they came to be there but Darlene said, "We got some business here with our strong young warrior." The Lakota man's expression was pained, but he did not try to break loose from the grasp of the women flanking him.

Mrs. K. spoke first and the room quieted to hear her. She craned her neck to address the man, not looking him in the eyes but making sure he knew he was the recipient of her words. She asked if he would give his name and he said she could call him Walker. "Thank you, Walker. We want to tell you directly what Mr. Chamisa here tried to but you did not want to hear it. The dream of buffalo and other things offers us, Indian people, an option. We don't have to take it. I think we will." She described how her cousins and friends in both Hopiland and on the Navajo side struggle to stay healthy and it's hard because most of the food is in Baxaba stores and makes people fat. "We Hopis grow a lot of our own food but we still have diabetes striking too many people."

Darlene took up the theme. "We got diabetes and there are drug problems and gang activity and some of our elderlies don't get the care they need so we've got many challenges. I think the buffalo coming back is us gaining our strength to live our lives like Navajos or Hopis or

Lakotas—wherever Indian people are, that's where we need to reclaim the strength of buffalos, don't you agree, tall man Walker?"

For a moment the Lakota activist was silent. He started to say something, lapsed again into quietude, and then began. "I did not mean to dishonor any of my brothers and sisters." He raised his forearms slightly and the women's hands rose and fell with the motion. "I respect what my grandmothers say here today, especially about being strong. Those are good words and I hope the P.R. guy up there—I hope Mr. Kee Chamisa will remember to say things about us Indian people going forward out of strength, a message we need to hear. And *keep* hearing"

Kee nodded. "That's right. I will. There are many ways for us to be strong and—" He paused, glanced at the Board members standing in a pensive semi-circle behind him. "Whatever we do for ourselves we do in the midst of folks from the white culture. I never heard anything from the Buffalo Dreamers that suggested anything except we are all in on this." He felt better, surer of the way forward, and his role in it, whether or not he remained as a spokesperson for the Council. He smiled lovingly at the two elderly women who retained their grip on the Lakota man. "Thank you, my grandmothers, for making the long and difficult journey here." Kee hesitated, then said, "Thank you, too, for coming here all the way from White River and for your words. I'll do my best to remember what you said. I might call you up and ask you for a quote now and then"

"Sure—I'll always have something to say." The Lakota man managed a smile and a disarming shrug. He left.

Sekia hugged Kee and he made his way through the throng of people and reporters to Darlene and Pauletta. He shook their hands with a light touch. "We got to get you some nourishment before you get back on that dog bus." The women exchanged amused glances. Darlene moved up to Sekia and affectionately curled her gnarled fingers around her forearm.

"When you called and asked if we could make the journey here you said we would be like elder fish, those salmon, who swim back up the stream from the ocean." Pauletta grinned and moved up to cup Sekia's other arm. "You *also* said if we could manage to get ourselves out here we could have a taste of wild strawberries and acorn bread and salmon like you make out here on the coast," Sekia assured the two women that she and her Aunt had prepared a little something in the way of a traditional Pomo meal.

Mrs. K beamed and replied, "That's good for us all. When the people grow and gather their food they gather and grow their spirit." The four nodded amiably and steadily made their way through the dispersing crowd, hungry as buffalo.

RC DEWINTER
ABRUPTION

you dropped me off
with the usual kiss
saying i have to go
i'll be loving you always

i watched the taillights
'til they were swallowed
by the corner
and went inside
hugging your warmth
like a shadow up and down
my length

and that apparently
was that

i feel myself fading
a bit more each day

soon i'll be nothing
but that walking shadow
strutting
fretting
feeding on the dust of dreams
and lines written to a ghost
that lives in pictures on a phone

a fool and her words
are soon parted

PRESTON SMITH
AFTER THE ARK

Forty days before the first meeting, forty nights
shivering alone

on waves with only your milky gray eyes
to wash down

the daffodils of those lost
to our storm—we never asked

for any reckoning, only existed
where we weren't allowed.

We bided our time but never hoped
for forty of anything was too much

to carry. Our families and friends tangoed
in thundercloud shadows, bit

floorboards with their steps. We were never sure
we would survive those nights

with only ghosts and no choice
but to accept imprisonment—*click*—

the temporal whir of feet on necks—
when the sun pulled me out

and dragged my feet through caking sand
I knew a new day was born.

TERRA VAGUS
APOCALYPSE

gusts of wind envelop any breath that may have been heard
as the dreamer
            gasps for air.

a new fear stamps out the ordinary drawbacks
of living
            outside of stagnant life.

the uneducated and ignorant sing hymns
composed of the sin
            they so proudly claim to live above.

a dreamer comes to a mirror
            with a higher risk of breaking.

rely on the left-behind guts of the gutless
to move forward in this life.
            rely on the brains of the brainless
            and you'll die of fright.

this state of affairs cannot be left behind.

it's in every corner,
            webpage and headline.

    break the mirror.

    keep the pieces.

seven years of bad luck
            isn't any different than this.

BRENDAN WALSH
LAO NEW YEAR

my students squat with small knives,
kill and gut fish after fish.
it's the hottest week of the year.

they speak to one another
about everything but death.
we lay the bodies on coal beds.

i eat the lungs of a catfish.
i eat the toothpick bones
of faceless riverine eel.

i'm a body made of bodies
made of bodies made of
bodies. i pass out and dream

of the mekong filling my throat.

Things My Mother Says

i.

He marries young, he's eighteen and she's seventeen. But his wife and sons and daughter hold him back from his life of partying and sleeping with other women. So they divorce. He remarries and starts a new family, and takes all of his kids to the circus together. His new daughter sits on his lap and I watch them laugh. I stare at him, holding his new daughter, and it hurts me. I think of the times I hid under the kitchen table when he came home drunk, swinging. I push my tongue into the roof of my mouth to cry silently. Tears well in my eyes and I watch the lion roar.

ii.

One day I'm working at the pharmacy and my father walks by. The storefront is glass and we make eye contact through it. He stops for a moment, he knows it's me but he continues walking. It hurts me but I like that he sees I became something. Both my brothers are like him, beautiful, smart, and athletic, throwing it all away for alcohol and cocaine.

iii.

I tell my brothers they have to be sober at my wedding, so one of them decides not to come. Rhode Island revokes his license for good and he goes to jail. I still give him money when he asks, even though I'm paying off your father's loans and a house for our family. If I don't give him the money he'll ask your grandmother, and I can't do that to her.

Things I Say

iv.

My mother tells me that story and I tell her she is selfless. She attributes it to faith—in God and her mother. Her mother has leukemia and thyroid cancer and is always working. She's always so sick but always so kind.

v.

My grandmother is remarried to a man who wears wigs and leaves violent porn in the VCR for my sister and me to find. I'll never tell her. Every time I call her we talk for hours and I love it but I don't have that kind of time anymore. And every time we're done talking she puts her husband on the phone and I think about the wigs and the porn and I hate it. I'm angry that men don't respect my grandmother. She thinks I don't call her because she's uneducated and not worth talking to. But it's not true. I don't know why I don't call. I wish I would. She is so lovely.

ANNA GENEVIEVE WINHAM
VACUUM

In early 21st century English there is a lacuna: there is no feminine equivalent for "guy." There are boys and *girls*, men and *women*, gentlemen and *ladies*. It is possible to say "guys and gals" if you push hard for these conjunctive phrases, but when a speaker says, "I'm meeting this guy," the feminine equivalent falls short. "I'm meeting this gal" has a hokey connotation not implied by the simple "guy." A guy is just an adolescent male. How do you describe an adolescent female?

There was an adolescent female who left a trail of broken keys all over Brooklyn. She warned people about this condition (it was involuntary, compulsive), yet people continued giving her keys, as though to say "I have faith you can change, o adolescent female," or, "I don't believe this is a real condition; this sounds like a neurosis of your own invention," (as though neuroses of one's own invention were therefore unreal!). The other component of her condition was that she always broke the keys in locks (she used the locks to break the keys), so it may be more accurate to say that she left a trail of broken locks, or even broken doors, all over Brooklyn. Here our 21st century English has provided us with a surplus of words to describe the same situation, and yet none of them precisely describes the exact state of brokenness.

The trail of broken locks, doors, or keys could certainly be interpreted as a physical manifestation of the adolescent female's broken interior. The trail could also be interpreted as the attempt to permanently open (or permanently break, or permanently lock) the doors of the hearts of the men she pursued. More practically, though, the broken locks left people trapped either inside or outside various rooms *or* in a state of relatively extreme uncertainty. I mean they couldn't lock their apartments. This meant that a significant number of people living in Brooklyn at this time had to leave their offices by climbing through windows. Neighborly relations became more intimate as a forced trust grew between leagues of residents with open residences. There were also more burglaries. The adolescent female was an accessory to a burglary in all these cases.

In jail, where no one gave her any keys, she finally kicked the habit. Well, she kicked one habit. Her attention turned, however, to "the prison that is language." Once again it was unclear whether a lacuna or an excess provided the lock or the key.

STEVEN RAY SMITH
BE THE COLOR OF YOUR BODY

A single heel step
from the door behind
so distinctly you
bubble friend
orange bubble
not to touch

In the dream you are
as purple as you are
leg to leg
sanguine diadem
stoplight mixed with midnight
through the window and negligee

Your subcutaneous hand
cannot be not
shaken each entry into
your white rotunda

If I'd met you without my eyes
you'd be red phosphorous
rivalrous allotrope
visible only in its test tube

Single sliver of shade in thickets of scrub sumac
you are the philosophical hue of a whole desert
ultimate terrain of the entire earth

ADAM MCOMBER
MARLOWE IN LOVE
Deptford, 1593

It was not Christopher Beaston, most famous of the boy actors, with pert lips and amber-colored eyes, who drew our Marlowe's attention. Nor was it Master Cook, nor Master Clarke, nor young Theopholis Bird, all of whom were known to expertly "play the illusion" when they donned the skirts and coiffed the hair. "These lads appear to lose their cods entirely," wrote George Weston in a private letter to the critic Roger Ascham. And it was true that Beaston and Cook and Clarke could, for a night, transform themselves, becoming Venus and Dido and even Kate the Shrew. John Rainolds, Puritan Father at Hampton Court, would warn of the "filthy sparkles of lust" such boys could engender with their "wanton gestures and bawdy speeches...kissing and bussing their way across the stage." But Marlowe himself paid little mind to either the boy actors or the Puritans. Nor was it the men who worked the brothels of Ram Alley and Little Sodom that drew good Marlowe's passion. The playwright was, of course, known to walk the streets at Whitehall and Seven Dials. He drank in taverns there and kept a certain company with the pale young men who wore their breeches tight. Marlowe flattered and teased, but never touched. Nor did he ask to see any such paramour in private rooms. Marlowe did not love red-haired Thomas Kyd with whom he lived in Shoreditch. He liked Kyd's writing well enough, all the blood and tongues and nails of it. But there was no tug between them. No heart that opened. There was one occasion where Marlowe and the young Master Shakespeare (another writer for the London stage) had a drunken contest in an alley behind Blackfriars. They agreed to fellate each other there. And the playwright who produced the most ejaculate would be declared winner. Master Shakespeare proved triumphant, giving Marlowe three mouthfuls of the stuff. And while the two admired each other well enough after that, no love ever bloomed. There was, in fact, only one man with whom Christopher Marlowe knew he would never be parted. And being the skilled diviner that he was, our Marlowe understood this man was not a proper body at all, but instead something like a shadow. Marlowe encountered him inside a dream. Red-caped Mephistopheles, that long-fingered devil, led the playwright deep into an earthy hole, and there Marlowe met a young man who looked very much like himself. Dark-haired and dark-eyed. A cleft upon his chin. The only difference between them was that this young man had a long-handled dagger sticking out of his right temple, silver blade thrust into his brain. Marlowe sat with the young man in the cave and they talked together. The playwright learned what it was like to be dead and murdered. And the young man learned what it was like to still be foolish and alive. At the end of a long night, the two—both no more than thirty years of age—fell asleep in each other's arms.

ARIEL SERENE
HANALEI HONEY

You press into me
and my brand new face
I am a masterpiece of honey
bound by bleeding lace

My hunter,
          What have you seen
          while I have wasted my years
          attempting to pick apart the light,
          to divide the Om,
          to set you down in my sleep.

I cannot help it. I fail for fun.
Perhaps wafting valerian
will lead me to air
in the hungry garden,
soldiers beg for sun
they cannot keep.
          I have not moved for a long time. I spill open in SURGERY
A certain un-wounded light, distilled and so warm,
inflates this empty space.

There is an
e m p t y s p a c e.

It is angry with color
          how quickly it fills with clairvoyant air

ADDITIONAL INFO

Follow us on social media:

@tildeliteraryjournal

@tildelit

/tildelit

Purchase a previous issue of Tilde~ at:

thirtywestph.com/shop

For full guidelines, submission info, and our
online archive, please visit:

thirtywestph.com/tildelit